Thierry Pastor

Oil addict

Argos Collection

Thierry Pastor: graduate in law and political science, he has been working as a political advisor for about fifteen years. Initially trained in politics, he specialized in the geopolitics of energy and global security. He has worked in several regions of the world, mainly in Eastern Europe and Asia. He is the co-author of several books on the geopolitics of energy, written with university professors, lawyers and economic intelligence specialists. He works in collaboration with several people with various skills: information systems, blockchain technology including cryptocurrencies, NFTs or metaverses. Thanks to this external expertise, these books were born.

From the same author

In the shadow of Titans, 2022

The dark power: the new weapons, 2022

Last chance, 2022

The limits of diplomacy, 2022

"True generosity to the future consists in giving everything to the present."
Albert Camus

"The Stone Age did not end for lack of stones, and the Oil Age will end long before the world runs out of oil."
Ahmed Zaki Yamani

Acknowledgements

This is curiously the first book I originally publish in French about oil before being translated in other languages. In the past, I had the opportunity to publish a dozen of them in English, for corporate purposes.

I warmly thank those who suggested me to write down these few thoughts about this mysterious and intoxicating world of oil. We adore it and we hate it. We cherish it and we curse it. Above all, it is found everywhere and at the heart of numerous political, economic, diplomatic, geopolitical, and geostrategic intrigues.

Thanks to you, my family, and my dear friends for convincing me to take up my pen. I had planned to write about black gold, but you were the motivational gas pedals. There is strength in numbers, and you have won me over! Thanks to you all.

I am deeply grateful to three people who have joined the wonderful LinkedIn adventure of *"Écrivains francophones, faites connaître vos oeuvres!"* This group has been in existence since September 2022 and has led to some wonderful encounters. Above all, it has allowed me to discover talented authors and engaging people.

To Stéphanie Bariet, a remarkable author and a wonderful storyteller that I invite you to discover without moderation.

To Jerry Galassi, the brilliant editor of the *Journal de la Next-Gen,* who has been kind enough to read my manuscripts before publication and give me his unvarnished opinions.

I also address a few words to Nicholas Beaulieu, the author of the masterful *Lawyers à la dérive* saga. I salute his talent as a writer, his witty character, and his always kind messages to me.

You cannot imagine the invaluable contribution you make by devoting your time to my writings and by clearing up some of my doubts that grow as the publication date approaches. Thank you very much.

Table of contents

Foreword

As I read the reports of the Intergovernmental Panel on Climate Change (IPCC), I notice a trend: each year they become more alarming. The scientists who contribute to the Panel's reports are constantly sounding the alarm. Climate change is of the utmost concern to them. Climatologists are pointing out disturbing weather phenomena. Natural disasters are occurring more frequently and increasing in intensity. For those who do not believe in global warming, temperatures are rising, indeed. In temperate zones, heat waves used to be rare. They are now tending to become more frequent. In France, I remember the one that hit the country in 2003. It was described as exceptional at the time. As for the polar regions, they are severely hit by increases in average temperatures that are not in line with seasonal norms. All of this seems to be a permanent feature, like an inevitability.

The Earth has always experienced climate change. These changes occurred naturally. Nowadays, one thing is clear: climate change is violent. It shocks by its intensity. During the last five decades, the rise in temperature has been meteoric. Moreover, it is in this same period that the growth in terms of consumption of hydrocarbons and oil has been the most significant. Linking oil consumption to global warming should not lead to the sole condemnation of black gold. It would be wrong to claim that hydrocarbons alone are responsible for this distressing situation. However, they do contribute to it. This means that human action is partly responsible for the rise in temperature.

In 2018, the average annual temperature was more than two degrees Celsius above that embodying the reference normal as defined for the period 1961-1990. [1]

Similarly, in 2017, global greenhouse gas emissions had doubled compared to 1970, but more importantly have grown by 40% since 1990. [2] As for oil consumption, what conclusion? It was 2,260 million tons in 1970. [3] In 1990, it peaked at 3,158 million tons and 4,662 million tons in 2018. [4] In other words, it has more than doubled between 1970 and 2018. It had accelerated sharply between 1990 and 2018, with an increase of almost 47%. These statements are not the ultimate proof of a clear correlation between global warming and oil consumption. However, their similar evolutions raise questions.

Every year, the scientific community is concerned about the overexploitation of natural resources. Each year, the "Earth Overshoot Day" is mentioned, the date on which humanity has exploited more than what nature generates in a year. Each year, this day comes earlier in the calendar. In 2021, the WWF association deplored that this day was reached at the end of July. [5] It is even more worrying that some of these natural resources are becoming scarce. This is precisely the case of oil. Yet we continue to overexploit it. Some people love it, adore it and worship it because it constitutes their wealth. Others denounce and loathe it because it embodies environmental deterioration and so many other evils. However, it is omnipresent. One denounces it and seeks to reduce one's dependence on it. State leaders agree that they want to reduce its consumption in favor of other less polluting energy sources. This discourse has been going on for several decades.

---

[1] *"Changement climatique et effet de serre,"* www.insee.fr, February 27, 2020

[2] *Ibid.*

[3] *"Consommation mondiale de pétrole de 1970 à 2018,"* fr.statista.com, 2022

[4] *Ibid.*

[5] *"Le jour du dépassement,"* www.wwf.fr, 2021

Nevertheless, its consumption does not stop growing. The gap between official good will and reality tends to grow.

Thus, what is one to make of this? Is there a barely concealed hypocrisy between the discourse and the concrete reality? For my part, I have been working with the energy sector for about fifteen years. I could be wrong, but I have the impression that the awareness of the leading political authorities is sincere and that there is a clear desire to reduce the international community's dependence on oil and, more globally, on fossil fuels. However, I defend the thesis that if the lure of profit remains unchanged, we are all aware that the future of life on Earth is threatened in the long term. The environmental damage is increasingly worrying. I fear that we will not be able to reduce this dependence because we are simply not capable of doing so, or at least not in the short term.

Today, the world's energy needs continue to grow for a variety of reasons including demographics and the emergence or economic confirmation of many national systems that are seeing their energy needs explode. New energies are being promoted but oil remains the most exploited resource. This is not without reason. Some economic issues are related to competitiveness. Others concern production capacity. But when we look at the issue of reducing oil consumption in the world in relation to energy needs, the question that comes to mind is: what will we replace it with? I wonder about the alternatives. I do not currently see which energy solution would significantly reduce dependence on oil. There are many studies and research conducted on the topic to find and develop the solutions of the future. However, in the current situation and at the risk of being misleading, I do not have the impression that the miracle solution exists. Indeed, it implies to find the remedy which will fill quantitatively the needs in oil; moreover, it would also be necessary that this last one is not harmful for the environment.

In my opinion, there is a big gap between the urgency of promoting energy solutions that will eventually replace hydrocarbons and what is likely to satisfy the world's energy demand without affecting the environment. The problem is far from being solved. I remain optimistic that energy solutions will be promoted soon and that they will hopefully prove to be less environmentally damaging. However, I hope that all this will not come too late because when I refer to the IPCC studies, I understand above all that we have no more time to wait. As for black gold, I would like to quote a famous Saudi statesman, Ahmed Zaki Yamani, who was his country's Minister of Oil and Mineral Resources for almost a quarter of a century: *"The Stone Age did not end because of a lack of stones, and the Oil Age will end long before the world runs out of oil."* Thus, according to its author, the age of oil will end because another energy will make the happiness of men. No doubt, but not in the immediate future.

Introduction

Since I was very young, I have been fascinated by the world of Tintin. One of the adventures of the famous Belgian reporter has always held my attention more than the others: *Land of Black Gold*. [6] I have always found this work captivating, perhaps because of its dramatic intensity. Throughout the story, the world fears the outbreak of war. At the heart of the stakes, spy intrigues but above all, oil in the background. Although this story was first published in 1950, Hergé conceived the scenario at the end of the 1930s, as the Second World War was approaching. He maybe knew how important black gold was even then. He probably had no idea that this resource would play a central role in the tipping point of the deadliest conflict in History.

For more than a century, naphtha has been the subject of much envy. There are a thousand and one ways to write about the topic. I have opted for a historical approach complemented by a geopolitical analysis, while striving to facilitate the understanding of the major interests that revolve around this raw material with such magnetic power. In the 20th century, it became the number one natural resource, the one that concentrated all the attention, the one that made Georges Clémenceau say that a drop of oil was equal to the value of a drop of blood. Since then, it has never stopped driving the world crazy. It bewitches some and frightens others. It has ensured the fortune of some and generated the distress of others. With oil, all tricks are allowed. One lies, one betrays, one kills for it. It must be recognized that those who felt the potential to be exploited did not have to complain about it. The American businessman John Davison Rockefeller built his fortune thanks to it and became the richest man in the world in his

---

[6] Hergé, *Land of Black Gold*, Casterman, 1950, 62 p.

time. His voracious appetite led to the Sherman Antitrust Act of July 2, 1890, a rule of law that gave birth to competition law. This legislation aimed to avoid any form of monopoly. However, John Rockefeller's fortune was such that despite the order to dissolve his Standard Oil in 1911, he still managed to become the major player in the new oil companies created in the United States. This man understood the benefits of oil before anyone else. Others understood it later, starting with the states.

During the 20th century, wars gave oil an ever-increasing role in international relations. Today, its strategic weight is such that the slightest disruption of international markets on production or supply causes cold sweats to any army chief of staff. An army without oil makes a country vulnerable. This natural resource thus has an equally important influence in international relations. The slightest annoyance linked to oil, its producers, infrastructure, or transport sets the world ablaze and sends it into turmoil. A simple announcement is sometimes enough to cause a panic in the financial markets. The omnipresence of black gold in contemporary international relations is such that, despite the desire of political leaders to move the world towards an era of decarbonization, it still has an influence on global economic life. The variations in its exchange prices are a precious indicator of the political and economic health of the planet. This is more remarkable for such a decried natural resource. Above all, it means that part of the global economic model is based on the oil market. Indeed, when this market is disrupted, a domino effect is immediately activated.

Oil is certainly one of the major international players of the 20th and 21st centuries. It played a major role in the Second World War. If Nazi Germany had won the battle of Stalingrad and managed to advance to the oil resources of the Caspian Sea, who knows how the war would have developed? Similarly, the post-war period was marked by the Cold War, an opposition between two blocs of states based on ideological dissonance. During this period, which spanned four decades, several jurisdictions with a common feature, the possession of opulent reserves of black gold, chose to join forces while world peace was severely threatened by the Washington-Moscow rivalry and the great European colonial empires saw many of the regions they administered take flight towards independence. The 1960s witnessed a new international geopolitical configuration more than ever disrupted by the creation of the Organization of the Petroleum Exporting Countries (OPEC) in 1960. The cartel quickly became a key player in the great global game, especially during this particularly critical context when periods of tension and détente followed one another. It brought together countries sharing the common will to show the world that they were sovereign over their oil wealth and that, given the importance of black gold in the world economy, their voice should be heard.

OPEC was never as powerful as it was in the 1970s and 1980s. It was during this period that the cartel shook the world with decisions that had far-reaching consequences for the global economy. In 1973, the first oil shock left its mark. The Yom Kippur War pitted the State of Israel against several Arab states. The producing countries of the Persian Gulf decided to considerably reduce their production of black gold. Saudi Arabia produced then more than 20% of the world's crude oil and imposed an embargo on its exports to the United States. The trading prices of black gold quadrupled in a short time. The economic growth of the major state powers of the time collapsed, generated mass unemployment, and other negative consequences.

In 1979, the fall of the Shah of Iran and the Islamic Revolution once again disrupted the international oil markets with a new surge in prices. This was the second oil shock. Meanwhile, the Cold War continued. The United States was clearly beginning to gain the upper hand over the Union of Soviet Socialist Republics (USSR), which was showing signs of losing steam. Ronald Reagan's famous Star Wars [7] had a serious impact on the Soviet economy, which was now trying to respond to the White House. In 1986, Moscow suffered two events that shook the precarious balance of the colossus with feet of clay. The Chernobyl disaster symbolized the irreversible decline of this state unit promoted by Lenin and proclaimed by the Treaty of Union of December 30, 1922. A few weeks later, the Soviet economy, already in its death throes, was hit hard by the collapse of oil prices. The USSR had hoped to generate significant revenues from its oil exports. However, amid the war between Iraq and Iran, both members of the OPEC cartel, Saudi Arabia implemented a policy of sharply increasing its oil production. It was followed by the other members of the organization. World supply then exceeded demand and trading prices collapsed. This strategy was intended to boost global demand for oil and boost Saudi revenues. In Riyadh, the gamble worked. On the other hand, it precipitated the irreparable fall of the USSR.

In the early 1990s, a new geopolitical order confirmed a paradigm shift in the balance of power within the international community. The end of the Cold War corresponded to the emergence and affirmation of a state power surpassing all others. With the collapse of the USSR, the United States no longer had any competitors capable of standing up to it. Meanwhile, after eight years of bloody warfare, Iraqis and Iranians ended their conflict. The

---

[7] Author's note: Nickname often given to the Strategic Defense Initiative policy promoted by President Ronald Reagan.

economic damage to both countries was considerable. Disappointed by the behavior of his creditors, Saddam Hussein began to put pressure on them, including Saudi Arabia and Kuwait. Feeling aggrieved, the Iraqi leader undertook to invade his Kuwaiti neighbor, which had the distinction of being full of oil reserves. Bad idea. The initiative was condemned by the international community, led by the United States. A broad coalition of thirty-five states intervened in the region to repel Iraqi troops. The aim of the maneuver was to show that not everything was allowed. Baghdad quickly understood its mistake, but too late. The so-called "fourth most powerful army in the world" at the time put up little resistance to the coalition forces. In the meantime, oil remained at the heart of the strategic issues of the day.

For the United States, the Middle East was a key issue, since most of its oil imports came from the region, particularly from Saudi Arabia. During the first Gulf War, the Wahhabi kingdom experienced internal upheavals that worried Washington and the White House then headed by George Herbert Walker Bush. These tensions stemmed from popular reactions denouncing the massive presence of American troops in Saudi Arabia, near the holy places of Sunni Islam. In the event of a possible regime change in Riyadh, the United States considered other options to secure its oil imports. Iraq's invasion of Kuwait provided the perfect opportunity to alleviate these fears. By defeating Saddam Hussein, the United States asserted its undisputed leadership of the world, which was reflected in the United Nations' sanctions imposed on Baghdad, including an embargo on oil exports. Meanwhile, despite continuing tensions with this Saudi neighbor, the United States continued to buy oil from its strategic partner since the alliance sealed by King Ibn Saud and Franklin Delano

Roosevelt, then the United States' Head of State, aboard the USS Quincy in February 1945.

In 2003, the United States again became involved in Iraq under different conditions than in the first Gulf War. Uncle Sam's country had suffered the attacks of September 11, 2001, in the meantime. The President in office, George Walker Bush, vowed to track down the culprits. The terrorist organization Al-Qaeda was behind these attacks. Most of the leaders of the organization were living in Afghanistan at the time, with the complacency of the Taliban regime. A joint military intervention took place in this Central Asian country... and lasted two decades.

Considering Iraq, the motives for intervention were much more obscure. Washington claimed a case of weapons of mass destruction. Inspections by the UN could never establish with certainty the possession of these alleged weapons by the regime still led by Saddam Hussein. Nevertheless, a joint military intervention, but with fewer state actors than in Afghanistan, took place in Iraq. Many people wondered why the United States was so keen to invest in Iraq when the famous weapons of mass destruction were probably a lie. One hypothesis emerged: the American neo-conservative influent actors might have intended to get their hands on Iraqi oil. Once again, this raw material was at the heart of suspicious issues. The official discourse justified the American intervention in Iraq through a fierce desire to fight against the dictatorship imposed by Saddam Hussein. Thus, it was important to democratize Iraq. As in Afghanistan, the international presence in ancient Mesopotamia dragged on. The operation to dethrone the irremovable dictator ended successfully. Yet the country fell into chaos. Two decades later, the Iraqi people still do not live in an environment of lasting social peace.

The 2000s were also marked by a remarkable evolution in international relations. The American ultra-dominance of the nineties seemed to be losing momentum in the face of China's growing economic power. The latter, discreetly, was then surfing on dynamic economic growth rates. Moreover, it was noted that the Middle Kingdom's oil needs were continually increasing in significant proportions. Clearly, was there a correlation between its economic performance and the steady increase in its oil needs? In the eyes of the American neo-conservatives, there was a connection. To curb China's economic dynamism, it was necessary to find a way to thwart Beijing's supply of black gold. In other words, oil was majestically at the center of the world economic leadership's concerns because the United States had clearly identified it as the real fuel for Chinese economic development.

Since then, China has continued its impressive economic development. As for its oil needs, it has grown accordingly, since it is now the world's largest importer of black gold. For several years now, it has made no secret of its ambitions to become the world's leading economic power. [8] The United States obviously does not see it that way.

As a result, China's oil needs have increased dramatically. When such a national economy sees its needs grow in this way, it does not go unnoticed in the world markets and the Middle Kingdom is far from being an exception. Many national economies in the world have seen their oil needs increase in this way. This is true for both the most favored and emerging economies. Thus, as mentioned in the foreword, world oil consumption has increased by almost 47% in just three decades. These ever-increasing

---

[8] Thierry Pastor, *"In the shadow of Titans,"* May 8, 2022, 208 p.

needs can be explained by the rise in world demographics, which has many consequences, since there are always more needs and services to satisfy. This in turn has an impact on industrial needs.

However, the calls to consider climate change are not recent. It is difficult to date the beginnings of this phenomenon precisely, but NASA researchers had already expressed their fears about possible global warming in the 1980s. They had then put forward a hypothesis stating a human responsibility in this phenomenon. In 1992, a UN event on the environment and development was held in Rio de Janeiro, Brazil. It symbolized the international community's awareness of climate change. On the UN website, the Rio Earth Summit is presented as follows: *"The Rio de Janeiro conference highlighted how different social, economic and environmental factors are interdependent and evolve together, and how success in one sector requires action in other sectors to be sustained over time. The primary objective of the Rio 'Earth Summit' was to produce a broad agenda and a new blueprint for international action on environmental and development issues that would help guide international cooperation and development policy in the twenty-first century."* [9]

In 1992, the international community had noted that the environment was deteriorating. The texts resulting from the Rio Summit [10] suggested that human activity was partly responsible. Commitments and objectives were defined to

---

[9] *"United Nations Conference on Environment and Development, June 3-14, 1992, Rio de Janeiro,"* www.un.org, accessed on July 6, 2022

[10] Author's note: The Rio Declaration and its twenty-seven universal principles, the United Nations Framework Convention on Climate Change, the Convention on Biological Diversity, the Declaration on Forest Principles, and so on. It was also at this event that the foundations were laid for other texts and conferences, including the creation of the Commission on Sustainable Development.

contain the problems identified as harmful for the environment. Thus, this conference marked a turning point. Everything had to be done to preserve the planet. Three decades later, bitterness characterizes the prevailing feeling regarding the evolution of the environmental state.

Since 1995, annual climate conferences under the aegis of the UN, the so-called COPs, have brought together numerous heads of state, government, and other international decision-makers. Each year, one reminds that it is imperative to act against climate change, although there are climate skeptics. One insists on the necessity to seize the bull by the horns in order not to further aggravate a global environment in a worrying state. Every year, when the IPCC submits its report, its conclusions are implacable. The more they insist on the urgency of containing the factors identified as generating climate change, the more the international community consumes what is at the origin of environmental ills. There is a yawning gap between the recommendations and decisions of the COPs and the conclusions of scientific studies.

Oil is not the only factor impacting the environment, but it is widely criticized because its use in industry and transport does indeed have undesirable effects on the environment. Above all, it is the subject of particular attention because the global economic model is partly based on its use. It remains at the heart of many strategic issues and represents an extraordinary financial manna. Unfortunately, it contributes to pollution and environmental deterioration. When public decision-makers advocate for the decarbonization of the global economy, black gold is necessarily in the crosshairs. In short, for many, the environment will be better off the day the international community does without hydrocarbons. That day has not yet arrived. To be able to envisage the gradual decarbonization of the world economy, alternative energy solutions must be available upstream. When one sees that the demand for oil has been rising steadily since the 1970s, except for a few one-off "accidents" such as Covid-19 recently, one must face the fact that if needs are growing, it is because one is not able to satisfy them in any other way than with oil... or because one does not want to do otherwise for other reasons.

In my opinion, although one is witnessing the promotion of other energy sources presented as less impactful for the environment, world energy demand is reaching such proportions that it is difficult to move towards a significant reduction in hydrocarbon consumption in the short term. Worse still, in Europe, given the events in Ukraine and the embargo imposed on Russian hydrocarbon exports, in the event of a prolonged crisis, some European countries would be forced to reopen coal-fired power plants. This has already been the case for other reasons, notably in Germany when Berlin ratified the cessation of all civil nuclear activity. However, the international energy reality reminds us of the difficulty to produce accordingly via renewable energies and other resources considered less impactful than oil for the environment to reduce its consumption. Secondly, there is certainly an economic issue. Naphtha generates considerable economic interests for producers, the financial sector and other actors who benefit from its economic spin-offs. It concentrates speculative stakes that can even jeopardize the global economic balance. This was the case in 2008 when the financial sector bet excessively on speculative products linked to oil which turned out to be particularly toxic. Nowadays, the war in Ukraine is once again encouraging high exchange prices. This is whetting the appetite of producers who have been languishing since 2015 with low selling prices, except for the United States, which has been doing well with shale oil that can be sold for less than so-called conventional oil... while ensuring comfortable margins.

Let's not fool ourselves: black gold, although designated as harmful for the environment, continues to be at the heart of multiple major issues. There will certainly come a day when it will be replaced by another energy resource, but in the meantime, it is still the focus of attention. Moreover, election promises are being reneged on for economic and strategic reasons. President Biden will not contradict this. During his victorious 2020 election campaign, he announced that he wanted to reduce oil production and focus more on so-called clean energy. After a year and a half of governance, it is unclear whether the United States is reducing oil production compared to the Trump era. Circumstances have meant that initial plans may indeed require revisions. Yet the number one U.S. executive has always made clear his intention to reinstate the country into the Paris Climate Agreement agreed at the 2015 Paris COP 21. Indeed, as soon as he arrived at the White House, his predecessor went out of his way to fulfill a campaign promise to withdraw Uncle Sam's country from this international agreement. For Joe Biden, it was important to make a firm commitment to the fight against climate change.

Since then, while the Covid-19 crisis persists, albeit less deadly than in its early days, global economic life is not as moribund as it used to be in 2020 and 2021. Demand for oil is on the rise again. In 2022, the escalation of tensions between Russia and the Ukraine cast doubt on the financial markets. They feared a conflict eruption and that a domino effect would occur, with all the hallmarks of a crisis that was both worrying and uncertain. The outbreak of hostilities has caused oil trading prices to soar above one hundred dollars per barrel of Brent or WTI. [11] Speculation has resumed in earnest. Fears are focused on production, supply, transportation, and other issues that could lead to a future imbalance in the world market. The imposition of an embargo on Russian hydrocarbon exports, first orchestrated by the United States and then by Europe, has contributed to maintaining a high trading price. For producers, such circumstances are unexpected: the sanctions against Moscow are reshuffling the deck on the world oil market. Moreover, the United States has perfectly understood the exploitable interest. Geographically distant from the Ukrainian conflict, it is doing excellent business by offering to supply its European allies with raw materials (primarily liquefied natural gas (LNG)) and reassuring them more generally that their fossil fuel needs will be met. Considering that the Ukrainian crisis will undoubtedly drag on and that during this time the economic sanctions against Russia will remain in place, the United States is ensuring that it will gain a good share of the European oil market. [12] American producers are not complaining. President Biden does not shy away from this advantageous business context as it is never a good idea to disappoint the U.S. oil lobby, especially when an important election date approaches. Indeed, the mid-term elections will be held in November 2022, while the general atmosphere in the United States dwells rather delicate due to numerous social ills that are undermining social peace, the latest example being the Supreme Court's decision to revoke the right to abortion. This conclusion deeply divides American society. In fact,

---

[11] Author's note: Brent crude oil is the main oil reference in Europe. It is extracted in the North Sea. West Texas Intermediate (WTI) is extracted in Texas and is the major reference for U.S. oil.

[12] Author's note: The implementation of the embargo on Russian exports has boosted demand for U.S. oil, particularly in Europe. By the end of February 2023, U.S. oil exports exceeded 5.5 million barrels per day, a record for the country.

Joe Biden himself has expressed his regret over the decision. In such circumstances, it is understood that the President of the United States knows how to rely on the right alliances or to satisfy the actors who could undermine his good governance. In this case, with such favorable barrel trading prices, why not help U.S. producers maximize their profits by facilitating their exports?

The difficulty of fighting climate change and the desire to decarbonize the world economy are partly based on political, economic, and more generally geopolitical interests that make oil the natural resource with the greatest power of influence, while officially seeking to reduce one's dependence on it. In a global environment where the depletion of oil reserves prefigures the hypothesis of a shortage of black gold that will not be compensated quantitatively in terms of volumes consumed by other energy resources, I am nevertheless firmly convinced that the era of oil will not come to an end because of the total exhaustion of this resource. It will happen the day the world economic model changes, the day when a new raw material or factor, not necessarily energy, takes the lead in terms of political, economic, geopolitical, or military influence. This is my vision. It is pragmatic. Despite the urgency to act against climate change, I have not become convinced that concerns about the future of humanity take precedence over the economic and political interests defended by the public and private decision-makers of this world. I conclude that Man is not yet done with his addiction to oil.

Some truths about oil

Everyone has heard of this natural resource, but one knows little about it. Many seemingly paradoxical truths surround it. For example, while some people associate oil with scarcity, others claim that there has never been so much naphtha on Earth. And yet, all this is true! A few explanations are in order.

Black gold is indeed becoming scarcer as soon as the volumes discovered each year remain lower than those consumed in the world. Because of this mathematical fact, oil is becoming increasingly scarce. However, proven reserves have never been so large. The French INSEE [13] defines them as *"[...] the quantities of hydrocarbons and coal which, according to the geological and technical information available, have a high probability (>90%) of being recovered in the future, from known deposits and under existing technical and economic conditions. This estimate is therefore continually re-evaluated based on new discoveries, price trends and improved recovery from existing fields."* [14] New oil discoveries are regularly made. Similarly, technological advances are making it possible to better detect deposits and, above all, to optimize their exploitation. As a result, proven reserves are on an upward curve. However, if the exhaustion of oil reserves does not

---

[13] Author's note: The INSEE is the French national institute of statistics and economic studies.

[14] Definition of *proven reserves* *"Réserves prouvées,"* www.insee.fr, October 13, 2016 Original version: *« [...] les quantités d'hydrocarbures, de charbon qui, selon les informations géologiques et techniques disponibles, ont une forte probabilité (>90%) d'être récupérées dans le futur, à partir des gisements connus et dans les conditions technico-économiques existantes. Cette estimation est donc continuellement réévaluée en fonction des nouvelles découvertes de l'évolution des cours et de l'amélioration de la récupération sur les champs existants. »*

yet seem to be on the agenda, one must keep in mind that humanity has exploited a good part of the Earth's oil in a century. In one hundred years, mankind has consumed most of a natural resource whose natural production process takes several tens or even hundreds of millions of years. This should be a cause for concern. Similarly, oil is not an exception since many natural resources suffer the same fate. However, these resources share the common characteristic of being exhaustible.

When I hear about the depletion of oil reserves, I wonder about the future of the planet and of humanity. Considering the speed at which mankind is exploiting the Earth's natural resources, for some of them, there is reason to worry because once they are exhausted, it will be preferable to have an alternative solution on hand. In the case of oil, I really wonder. There are certainly alternatives. However, to date, given the world's consumption of black gold, I do not know what would allow us to replace a large part of the current oil needs in the short term. In saying this, I have not even entered the debate on climate change and the need to turn to energy solutions that have less impact on the environment. I will come back to that later. I really wonder about the legacy my generation will leave to its children. I believe in the thesis of a climate change for which Man holds a large part of the responsibility. Although this thought is not unanimous, climate disruptions have been observed and are probably not due to chance or to natural causes alone. The abundant use of oil is certainly not unrelated to these disturbances or malfunctions which make certain natural phenomena more frequent, and which are sometimes accompanied by natural disasters of devastating intensity. Oil is obviously not responsible for everything, but it is iconoclastic because its importance in the world economy and politics has reached such heights that I sometimes wonder if the Earth does not revolve around a big barrel of crude oil... I will not enter philosophical considerations postulating that Man appreciates easy solutions or that he easily gives in to comfort, wealth, and other appreciable living conditions. No, this is not the spirit of this reflection. Oil can be undeniably associated with progress. However, its over-consumption is now proving to be detrimental to the planet, in more ways than one.

Black gold is a natural resource known since ancient times. However, it took more than two millennia for it to become a widely exploited resource and a wonderful treasure for those who knew how to take advantage of it. Like many other natural resources, its exploitation and consumption have exploded in the last century. Several factors allow us to understand this increase, first progressive then exponential, of the needs to be satisfied and requiring more and more natural resources.

Initially, the industrial revolution of the 19th century transformed the national economies of the main state-owned engines of the time. Since then, technological, and industrial progress has unquestionably resulted in an explosion of natural resource needs. Industrialization has made it possible to produce in large quantities and in a short time. Consequently, it was necessary to supply industries with raw materials. Oil has not escaped this trend, except that its properties began to be understood after the industrial revolution. The day that some entrepreneurs started to see the advantages of oil for the developing industries that cannot do without black gold, the demand for oil has never stopped growing since then. This trend has been confirmed by industrial and technological advances, as mentioned above, but not only. Since naphtha was first used for industrial purposes, the world's population has grown dramatically, from 1.5 billion in 1900 to nearly 8 billion nowadays. In the meantime, a host of new consumer goods and services has marked social developments over the past century. Above all, it has given rise to an explosion in the need for raw materials, including oil, which one finds in so many sectors of activity.

Black gold is turning heads. Although it is now designated as one of the enemies to be fought in the framework of the energy transition, it will not be so simple to get rid of it. In fact, the situation seems rather distressing. Indeed, the more we hammer away at the need to reduce our dependence on oil and promote other energies, the more its worldwide consumption increases! Look for the error! I would remind you that the scientific community's concerns about climate change are not new. For more than three decades, it has noted a progressive deterioration of the environment while at the same time it has noticed an acceleration of the denounced problem comparable to the increase in the volume of oil consumed in the world. All this led the UN to organize the famous Earth Summit in 1992. The UN agenda was then undoubtedly also motivated by the Gulf War that occurred between August 1990 and February 1991. One still remembers the images of Kuwaiti oil wells set on fire by Iraqi troops, which generated unprecedented air pollution. It took the famous fireman Paul Adair and his teams more than six months to extinguish nearly one hundred and twenty burning wells. I remember the images of thick plumes of black smoke that filled the news at the time.

When one associates black gold with pollution, one also thinks of oil spills. As soon as an oil tanker leaks large volumes of oil into the seas and oceans, there is considerable environmental damage. The same applies to problems of leaks from offshore pipelines. In 2010, the incident on the Deepwater Horizon oil platform in the Gulf of Mexico left a lasting impression. Eleven people died when the site exploded. Similarly, although it remains difficult to assess the precise volume of oil that contaminated the ocean, it is estimated that eight hundred million liters had been spilled. This was equivalent to five million barrels of oil contaminating the ocean and causing an environmental disaster. As for the oil major BP, the company that leased the platform in question, it was subjected to a judicial thunderbolt after several years of investigation and proceedings with a record of fine penalties. It was necessary to make an example of it.

These incidents remain rare. However, the environmental inconvenience caused by the intensive use of oil is much more significant when it comes to industrial needs, transportation and other sectors that require this natural fossil resource. And what about the behavior of human beings? When dealing with environmental degradation, let's not hide behind air pollution alone! In just a few decades, one has managed the prodigious feat of polluting the soil and the seas! Once again, oil finds itself in the crosshairs of those who denounce its unfit properties for the environment. Don't see any irony in this! The tone is meant to be sarcastic because it is easy to forget that part of the marine pollution comes from incivilities that one commits daily. Discreetly throwing away a cigarette butt, a bag, or a plastic bottle, all of this constitutes harmful behavior for the marine ecosystem. But many do it! Plastic products are a magnet for criticism. Bad luck for them, they are derived from oil! Ask fish, seabirds, dolphins, or turtles, I think their organisms do not appreciate ingesting plastics. This is dramatic. On a global scale, there is the equivalent of a continent of plastic in the oceans. Desert islands are being invaded by plastic waste. An article published in *National Geographic* had exposed the case of Henderson Island. [15] The latter is located halfway between New

Zealand and Chile. For the geography lovers, it is one of the islands composing the Pitcairn State. Imagine in this Southern part of the Pacific Ocean this natural space soiled by several tens of millions of wastes, a large part coming from plastic elements. In most cases, this waste should never end up in the sea.

Oil is harmful to the environment. It is even more regrettable when it emanates from avoidable and disrespectful incivilities. For many reasons, quite justified by the way, the intensive consumption of oil and its by-products generates undesirable and unwanted effects for the planet. However, as already indicated, the more one denounces its extensive use, the more one consumes it! But on closer inspection, there is nothing surprising about this apparent paradox. Black gold has ensured the fortune of many public and private economic actors. It has the double advantage of being abundant and easily exploitable at an acceptable cost compared to other natural resources. Consequently, it has become the easy option, which also has the extraordinary property of being profitable. From this point of view, one has been witnessing for several decades a kind of golden goose syndrome. A gigantic natural treasure has allowed its owners and operators to lay the world at their feet. Its economic importance and its power of influence in the field of international relations have reached dizzying levels. It is therefore not surprising that oil has a dominant position in the world's energy mix, especially as its global demand has steadily increased. This is also true for the other fossil resources, natural gas, and coal. I claim to have a realistic view of international relations. If I am not negative in my thinking, I try to present pragmatic analyses. In this case, the fight to decarbonize the world economy is

---

[15] Laura Parker, *"38 Million Pieces of Plastic Trash Cover This Remote Island,"* www.nationalgeographic.com, May 17, 2017

urgently needed. Nevertheless, let me express some personal thoughts on the topic.

First, a normative dynamic has been effectively promoted in recent years to define and achieve quantified decarbonization objectives. Europe is fully committed to this approach. Other sources of energy, presumed to be less polluting, are now presented as future alternatives, such as hydrogen. I personally believe in it. I trust that scientific and technological progress will enable us to produce energies capable of replacing the needs currently met by oil... but not soon. The European institutions are certainly right to set high targets for decarbonization, but the energy transition will take several decades. One cannot imagine what such a program will entail in terms of investments in research and development, infrastructure, transportation and other necessary but considerable expenses.

Second, I dread the transition phase insofar as I do not see any alternative energy source being produced in sufficient quantity, in the short term, to drive a significant decrease in oil consumption. Similarly, the engineering world will criticize me, and rightly so, for not being able to debate the pollution generated by future energy solutions, but I would like to see evidence that these supposedly "cleaner" solutions are indeed cleaner. Until proven otherwise, any transformation induces particles. Beyond this consideration, one should already find a way to considerably reduce the share of fossil fuels in the global energy mix in a short time... preferably. This is a major challenge.

Third, while the economic model of many companies is being impacted by the desire to decarbonize the global economy, many countries still have a national economic model that is partly based on the exploitation, sale, or consumption of fossil resources. Thus, I wonder: will everyone digest the energy transition well? I regularly observe and learn about those states that have relied on oil, natural gas, and coal for several decades. I come back to the image of the goose that lays the golden egg. When one owns such a treasure, one wishes to make the most of it. This vision induces an economic dependence of the country on the exploitation of these resources and that the other sectors of activity are not sufficiently developed. The same is true for consumers. I hope I am wrong, but I fear that some people will mismanage the end of this economic providence. Any form of dependency dwells potentially dangerous. The countries concerned only must diversify their economic activity, should be opposed to this assertion. Of course! I would indeed advise them to do so... but it is not that simple. To diversify, one needs to attract, finance, and ensure positive spin-offs. But for the oil kings, one often forgets that these countries are exposed to threats that could destabilize their political, economic, and social life. In fact, when one looks at the statistics for the largest holders of proven black gold reserves, these countries are experiencing numerous internal upheavals, such as Venezuela, Iraq, Libya, and Iran. Others must deal with an uncertain and potentially damaging regional environment to attract foreign investors. I am thinking of the rich oil-monarchies of the Arabian Peninsula, led by Saudi Arabia.

The Saudi case is interesting because the country is experiencing a resurgence in economic form now that oil trading prices are again flirting with record highs. The national economy has been severely strained in recent years. This has shown, above all, that the Wahhabi kingdom remains essentially dependent on its oil rents, which can quickly become problematic when exchange prices fall or collapse. The Crown Prince is optimistic and ambitious. He advocates the need to turn to other sectors of activity that can generate wealth. But will he succeed? Saudi Arabia embodies the image of excess, that of a rich oil player enjoying the luxury of promoting the most extravagant and allegedly avant-garde projects which lead to pharaonic investments. As a reminder, the country's economic model is based on the rents earned by Saudi Aramco, the national company that exploits hydrocarbons. When the price of black gold fell in the 2010s, dark clouds began to gather over the heads of local policymakers. The private sector was not well developed in the country. The economic model was running dangerously low, while most of the country's population was under the age of thirty. The Wahhabi kingdom was also at the heart of regionally sensitive geopolitical issues and concerned about the ongoing war in Yemen. It became imperative for Riyadh to change course in terms of its economic model and to reduce the country's dependence on oil rents. To do this, it was necessary to modernize its national economic model. It involved developing the private sector and attracting foreign investors. In absolute terms, the plan seemed simple, but one should never trust appearances! If the local authorities are now trying to promote their country and invest massively in sectors of activity that they consider promising, such as tourism and education, will the future wealth generated by this economic diversification make up for the shortfall caused by a presumed drop in oil activity, assuming an effective reduction in world oil consumption? For this to happen, Riyadh will have to find effective channels to compensate for what currently provides the bulk of the national GDP. In view of the rather uncertain regional context, the country will undoubtedly try to attract foreign investors by offering them advantageous investment conditions. However, will this be enough to allow for a significant decline in oil revenues to be offset by revenues from other sectors? Only time will tell.

The Saudi case is no exception. It is said that money does not make one happy. This is especially true with black gold. In fact, there is a relatively unhealthy climate around the oil world. Those who have direct access to this natural resource hope to maximize their business through trading and speculation. One might as well say it, all the tricks are allowed! The actors who have an interest in selling it do not hesitate to play on the fear effect to try to influence the exchange prices upwards. They communicate in this sense. One plays on emotions. Doubts, uncertainties and even threats are raised, for example, about the state of real reserves, while some are producing more than they officially declare to be able to sell off the beaten track. However, all these maneuvers have short-lived or limited effects on the financial markets, as trading prices are the result of many factors that blur the effects of these unethical maneuvers. However, those who do business with oil have every interest in claiming that it is running out, that it is becoming scarce. In economics, scarcity comes at a high price. This is precisely the ambiguity of the oil sector. It is said to be scarce when others claim the opposite. What is the real situation? As I have already briefly mentioned, there are a few "truths" that are still poorly understood or explained. When one talks about scarcity, it is a mathematical approach. When one consumes more than one discovers, this inevitably induces a tendency to rarefaction. On the other hand, another reality is too often overlooked, namely the technological and technical progress that has made it possible to further optimize the exploitation of deposits. Although one is considering a natural resource that is exhaustible, one is not yet at the point of sounding the alarm and threatening to exhaust the available reserves. Nevertheless, for environmental purposes and to protect the international community against this future risk of depletion, it is especially important to anticipate the disaster scenario of a lack of alternative solutions.

World wars, oil, and growing influence in international relations

Polemology characterizes the branch of international relations specialized in the study of conflicts. When one studies the wars that marked the 20th century, one actor, sometimes discreet, sometimes at the heart of the intrigues, plays the role of the common denominator: oil. This natural resource has marked its time to the point of being omnipresent and unavoidable, of favoring victories or precipitating failures, of strengthening the power of some or leading to the decline of others. Above all, it has shaped the history of the last century, the one of large-scale conflicts, of the most consequential human losses ever recorded, of the logistical means and the more sophisticated and destructive weapons ever used. This century of barbarism would probably never have taken such a tragic dimension without oil. It has been linked, in one way or another, to every major crisis since the outbreak of the First World War. No other natural resource has caused as much excitement as what is known as black gold, this oil compared to the much sought-after precious metal. Nothing frightens as much as a hypothetical risk linked to a disruption in the production, transport and more generally the accessibility of oil. It is systematically at the heart of the great concerns of our time.

However, times have changed as technology has advanced. An adversary can be attacked remotely without the use of armed forces. A well-executed cyberattack can be extremely damaging to its victim. Imagine the remote hacking of a nuclear power plant. This is not a science fiction scenario. Despite this, oil remains a central player in international relations. Like an octopus, it has multiple tentacles spread across numerous sectors of activity as well as in the arcane of the great political, geopolitical, and geostrategic intrigues of this world, all of which are closely interconnected.

March 2023, the French government tries to force through a bill on pension reform but encounters vehement political and social opposition. For several weeks, debates have been raging in Paris and in the provinces. Social movements disrupt the smooth running of national economic life. Some fear the birth or return of a movement inspired by the Yellow Vests. A general and lasting mobilization could indeed lead executive decision-makers to opt for a retro-pedal if it were to take on sufficiently worrying proportions in terms of public order and its economic repercussions. However, if there is one threat that the Elysée Palace [16] and the Hôtel de Matignon [17] fear, I bet it is oil and the strikes in the refineries. Although France has strategic stocks, a lasting social movement leaves the image of a sword of Damocles hanging over the heads of its public decision-makers. A country without oil becomes a terribly vulnerable territory, open to a domestic crisis that will proliferate at great speed. An oil shortage condemns transport users, the industrial world, and the army. It paralyzes a country and its people. In such a case, this type of crisis quickly becomes a snowball effect that the executive power must apprehend at the risk of being submerged by its consequences. In this case, oil plays the role of pressure tactic par excellence because it constitutes the ultimate threat of the social and economic paralysis of a country. In some respects, this description is akin to taking the nation hostage, since not all social actors agree on how to put pressure on the government's pension reform project. As I write these lines, this theme makes the headlines in the French media and constitutes the subject of political speculation aimed at unseating the government through a

---

[16] Author's note: Official residence of the French Head of State
[17] Author's note: Official residence of the French Prime Minister

vote of no confidence. Beyond the potential political consequences for the executive power, the fact remains that black gold is brandished as a real means of pressure. The media relay information about gas stations that are out of stock. The more the announcements are oriented towards a lexical field mentioning possible large-scale shortages in the making, the more the ambient climate will become anxiety-provoking. What can be done for those who depend on their vehicle to go to work, to do their shopping, to take and pick up their children at school or other indispensable tasks of their daily life? Without gasoline in the engine, many will quickly find themselves embarrassed or even disoriented, like the user of a cell phone that they have just lost or cannot use for an indefinite period. In other words, if oil is not vital, people depend on it considerably for the essential actions of their daily life and for their comfort. However, any threat of a shortage of black gold acts as a stimulus for everyone to fear the worst. One does not mess around with oil! When I associate our precious oil with the adjective *vital*, I plead guilty to a deliberate heresy because it is obviously not comparable to Man's need to access water to live. Without water, there is no life possible. Without oil, Man can live, although its inaccessibility can quickly become disruptive and damaging to him. However, the difference remains fundamental.

This reflection leads me to consult the abundant media news on the subject. In this case, the IPCC has just published a summary of its last six reports. Unsurprisingly, it does not bring any reassuring news. Very briefly, it states that the temperatures recorded on Earth over the period 1970-2020 have not increased in the same way for over two thousand years. [18] Similarly, when one considers the emissions of greenhouse gases produced since 1850 and the

---

[18] IPCC, *Urgent climate action can secure a liveable future for all*, www.ipcc.ch, March 20, 2023

beginnings of the industrial era, nearly half have been emitted since 1990. The IPCC specifies that to limit global warming and that it does not exceed 1.5 ° C compared to pre-industrial levels, one must halve greenhouse gas emissions ... by 2030. [19] The alarm bells were once again rung in Interlaken, Switzerland. Scientific common sense insists on the need for immediate and effective action, otherwise the planet will be precipitated into a situation of no return in terms of climate consequences. The higher the temperature rises, the more the crucial question of access to water will arise. I still catch myself naively dreaming of a better world in which one would seize the bull by the horns to avoid any fatal scenario. The winter has barely ended in France and many regions are already suffering from drought and are subject to restrictive water use measures. The IPCC keeps on hammering that Man is acting like gravedigger. However, not everyone understands the issue of climate change with the same seriousness.

When I write that oil does not have a vital function for Man, its overconsumption can nevertheless lead to its loss. I persist in reminding you that it should not be designated as the only factor impacting the environment, even if when checking the IPCC statistics on temperature readings, greenhouse gas emissions and the periods concerned, the observation becomes implacable: everything is consistent with the continuous increase in the consumption of black gold in the world. As mentioned in my foreword, oil consumption has more than doubled worldwide between 1990 and 2018. Fingers are pointed at the massive consumption of fossil resources, and the Earth's people are warned that if they continue in this direction, they will soon be exposed to irreversible natural disasters and consequences that will be detrimental to their existence.

---

[19] *Ibid.*

In short, as soon as one starts talking about the decarbonization of the world economy, one is obviously venturing into familiar territory from *Dallas* and its unforgiving universe. Despite all the talk about black gold, the sacrosanct oil has not finished pouring onto our planet. Man does not need it to ensure his life on Earth; nevertheless, he has set it up as an inescapable value of a standard he has created: the economic system. This is how it has become an influential player in international relations and how its importance has grown to unsuspected proportions. While there are fears about the depletion of the world's freshwater reserves and the threat to sustainability on Earth, I feel that oil is being given a higher dimension. The secret of the strength of this precious oil lies in its extraordinary magnetism on the contemporary economy and its primary military necessity. If I translate this sentence into a more familiar vocabulary of international relations, black gold is inevitable in *hard power* and *soft power*. [20] There is currently no competitor that can challenge its title as the most influential natural resource in international relations and global economy.

I deliberately ignore the causes that contributed to the outbreak of two of the deadliest conflicts in history and

---

[20] Author's note: *Hard power* and *soft power* are theories of international relations. They originate from Joseph Nye. A prominent political scientist and author of numerous internationally recognized books and articles, he was Assistant Secretary of Defense for International Security Affairs under President Clinton from 1994 to 1995. He defends the thesis that *hard power* is characterized by the traditional means of pressure within the political and military power relations. *Soft power* is based on a more subtle and flexible power of influence. It can be translated into economic or cultural policies. With Robert Keohane, he founded neoliberal institutionalism, a theoretical vision of international relations in which the power of institutions is great in the international system. Joseph Nye is one of the great names in international relations theory and one of the prestigious references of liberal thought.

focus on the immense role played by our beloved oil during and after these wars. Men bet so much on it that it periodically monopolized the attention of the international community during several stormy episodes of the Cold War. When nuclear energy was not a preoccupation during the tensest periods of East-West opposition, black gold became the instrument of disorder par excellence, the instrument of demands that were listened to carefully. No one took lightly the threat of future disruptions in the production of the world's major producers, with OPEC in the lead. The past century is full of examples of how oil has been a pervasive influence into the third millennium. It has been so prominent that I do not hesitate to call it the "absolute star of the century". Don't see any irony or exaggeration in that! I cannot think of any other disruptive element that has been so closely linked to the great political and economic affairs of the 20th century.

When one studies the First World War in depth, the works of Erich Maria Remarque or Roland Dorgelès show the horror of the trenches, the daily life of these millions of individuals delivered on the altar of the most unbearable human barbarity. For four years, Men fought relentlessly. More than eighteen million dead, soldiers, and civilians, as many wounded, that is the dark balance sheet that characterized the peak of inhumanity to which so many state belligerents gave themselves up. Never had a war killed and bruised so many on such a large scale. When the actors of the Treaty of Versailles signed the said document on June 28, 1919, they sought to save the world from another abominable butchery of the kind. They made a point of establishing a new world order that would give pride of place to the victors. The outcome of the First World War marked the end of the Western empires: Prussia, Austria-Hungary, Russia, and the vast Ottoman Empire collapsed forever. Numerous new states came into being.

On the victorious side, new responsibilities were negotiated in territories that had previously been under the authority of losers. The Middle East was divided up like a cake. The British got the best of it, without question. Understand that they won the prize by placing their pawns in oil-rich lands. The post 14-18 period conditioned in large part the course of the century. All the major oil deals were the result of the conditions agreed in Versailles. However, to the credit of the negotiators, no one imagined that the world would once again sink into the horror of 1939 to 1945, that several major players in the Great War would fall into experiments in severe authoritarianism, even totalitarianism in the case of Hitler's Germany and the Stalinist USSR. On the other hand, the winners of Versailles took care to look after their economic interests, for which oil was no stranger. Moreover, the latter acquired its letters of nobility during the great battles opposing the Triple Alliance and the Triple Entente. Without oil, one could not win. For the first time, technological advances requiring products derived from black gold to function were used. Tanks, warships, and fighter planes gobbled up huge volumes of foul-smelling oil. If the collective memory retains the image of the battles fought from the famous trenches, the air force, the navy, and the armored divisions played an essential role in the outcome of the war. For that, it was still necessary to have access to the oil fields and to control the production areas.

The occurrence of the First World War caused the need for oil to skyrocket... and its price. The latter increased considerably. It was therefore important that the means of production satisfy this consumption imperative or else the unsatisfied camp in need of black gold would lose ground to its adversary. For the first time, oil was dressed up in a suit of lights and haunted the concerns of the strategists of the time. Without it, a final victory could not reasonably be expected. Two decades later, it was an unostentatious reminder that any ambitious warmonger had to secure the necessary supplies upstream. To set out to conquer oil in the East while hostilities were already raging in Western Europe was akin to scuttling. The armies of the Third Reich learned this the hard way. Nazi Germany had its eye on the oil reserves of Azerbaijan. It was therefore necessary for it to attack its ally Stalin and violate the German-Soviet non-aggression pact signed in 1939. Adolf Hitler probably never imagined that he would get involved in such an infernal quagmire. The Red Army faced immense human losses. The USSR suffered severely from the German invasion, which in the end never succeeded in achieving its objectives: reaching the Baku region and its black gold reserves. The fate of the Second World War changed. Once again, the leader who could not satisfy his oil needs to feed his armies exposed himself to an increased risk of military defeat.

Oil was not the only factor explaining the German defeat in 1945. It did, however, upset Berlin's plans to lose control of operations in the East and had negative consequences on the Western Front. The German armies needed considerable volumes of black gold, which they hoped to draw from the Baku region. This scenario never happened, as they did not advance beyond Stalingrad, the present-day city of Volgograd, several hundred miles away from the coveted Caspian oil fields. The long battle of the same name marked a turning point in the war because of the human losses suffered by Germany and its allies. [21] As for

---

[21] Author's note: The Battle of Stalingrad lasted more than six months, from July 1942 to February 1943. It caused more than four hundred thousand deaths on the side of Germany and its allies, nearly five hundred thousand within the Soviet troops. As for the civilian population, historians estimate its losses at one hundred thousand. Taking all sides together, including the civilian population, this sad episode of the Second World War claimed nearly two million dead or wounded victims.

the morale of the troops, it was undermined. The main consequence was the retreat of the Reich's armies and their entry into a downward spiral of defeat. On the Soviet side, Stalingrad sealed forever the survival of the USSR and a new military momentum that was punctuated by the capture of Berlin in 1945. The quest for Caucasian oil was a determining factor during events of the Second World War... and the years that followed.

What would have happened if the German armies had triumphed at Stalingrad? Would the Reich have won everything in the East and in the West? No one knows. On the other hand, the USSR would probably have collapsed in such a scenario. Thus, there would never have been a Cold War between the Communist bloc and its former Western allies in the twilight of the Second World War. This is not to say that there would not have been acute tensions between the United States and the presumed dominant Germany in Europe in the event of a final Berlin victory. When one considers the chronology and the course of past events, the battle for oil certainly and negatively impacted the plans devised by Adolf Hitler. At the end of the Battle of Stalingrad, a milestone had been reached. Germany was no longer to march on Europe as it had done since the outbreak of hostilities in 1939. The desire to lay hands on the Caspian black gold won out over the excessive ambitions of a dictator resolutely driven by the denial of reality and the gravity of events. From Moscow, the German debacle was savored. The war was deadly and costly, but it was important to put Adolf Hitler out of action. Everyone knows what happened next. The war continued until 1945 and the surrender of Germany. However, the great maneuvers had begun before the end of hostilities. The United States, the United Kingdom and the USSR had already begun discussions as early as 1943 and the Tehran conference. A new and uncertain world order was being shaped. The bombing of Hiroshima and Nagasaki in August 1945 made the atom a new power in international relations. It caused much turmoil in the world during the four decades of the Cold War. Oil was quieter, but it was not forgotten. Unlike the atom, it played an essential role in the outcome of the long political crisis that saw the collapse of the USSR and the disappearance of the communist bloc.

After the Japanese surrender on September 2, 1945, the Second World War officially ended. For six years, it opposed numerous states, some of which were assisted by their colonial empires. Never had a war involved so many people and so many logistical resources. Never had a war killed and destroyed so much. It was necessary to get back on one's feet and make sure that one did not repeat the mistakes that had been made after the end of the First World War. Lasting peace was then obvious. However, between what seems logical or necessary and what happens, there is sometimes an abyssal chasm. The Cold War was looming. A new era of international relations was beginning, while another movement was taking shape in various parts of the world, the desire for emancipation expressed by peoples under foreign rule: decolonization. This was a great deal for an international community that was still licking its festering wounds inherited from the Second World War. Above all, it was seeing new areas of crisis erupt and shake the certainties of the main European colonial powers. In short, the post-war period saw the world split in two, like a mathematical plane characterized by the abscissa and ordinate axes. East and West engaged in ideological opposition, while North and South were torn apart over the independence of new states. All these new tensions had a strategic dimension related to oil. Black gold did not necessarily appear to be the primary explanation for these ills, but it was strangely never far away! Between economic growth and the need to secure oil supplies to support it, this raw material appeared more than ever as one of the central elements of post-1945 international relations.

45

Black gold during the cold war

The greatest human ignominy in world history officially ended on May 8, 1945, in Europe. A few weeks later, the Potsdam Conference brought together the three great victors of the Second World War: the United States, the USSR and the United Kingdom. Unlike Yalta, where Stalin, Churchill and Roosevelt met, only the Soviet Generalissimo participated in the German event of July 1945. Roosevelt died in April of the same year and Truman received the honor of succeeding him while the war was continuing in Europe and the Pacific. As for Churchill, although he was very popular in the United Kingdom, he suffered an electoral defeat in the general election that brought Clement Attlee to the forefront. Winston Churchill, for his part, continued to warn the Western world of Stalin's hidden agenda, which was to encourage the rise to power of Communist parties in Eastern Europe. Little by little, the allies of yesteryear drifted apart to give rise to this four-decade long episode known as the Cold War. This umpteenth dark period of the 20th century was about an ideological confrontation as well as about the race to the atom... but also about the control of oil and more generally everything that had a link with this so precious oil. In other words, one must understand that new geopolitics of this coveted sesame was set up according to the events of the Cold War. Thus, the pipeline networks or the control of the straits became as important as the government of the oil fields. While some wars were fought based on ideology and interposition [22], others saw black gold occupy an almost

---

[22] Author's note: During the Cold War, the term "conflict by interposition" was used to describe the fact that the USSR and the United States never directly confronted each other on the military field. When one side engaged in an armed conflict, the other supported the opposing side. Thus, the Vietnam War saw an American intervention while local opponents received Soviet aid. In Afghanistan, the opposite

central role among the explanatory causes. When one combines ideological opposition, the race to the atom and the redrawing of the world amid decolonization, all that is missing is oil to make the pressure cooker's lid quiver. All this happened in the fifties and sixties. But in September 1960, a newcomer on the international scene disturbed the great world political game even more: OPEC. As one can see, between the beginning of the Cold War and the early 1960s, fifteen years passed during which numerous conflicts and other tensions broke out in all four corners of the planet.

One crisis in particular catches my attention: Iran. Not only did it have its share of emulators, but it showed to what extent the stakes relating to black gold exacerbated the East-West rivalry to the highest degree. At the beginning of the 1950s, the country experienced internal turmoil that was greatly influenced by external actors, particularly the British and the Americans. They had figured prominently since they were exploiting the local oil. On March 15, 1951, Prime Minister Hossein Ala promoted the nationalization of the country's oil industry, which the British government promptly declared illegal. When I mentioned the East-West and North-South tensions, Iran fit perfectly into this double issue. On the one hand, the country was seeking to free itself from any form of external domination, especially economic. It therefore had to regain control of what assured it important sources of revenue while working with foreign partners who knew how to exploit them. On the Western side, the Iranian attitude provoked the anger of London and Washington because not only were their economic interests threatened, but Iran also shared borders with the USSR. In other words, there were fears of a strategic rapprochement between Moscow and Tehran. Meanwhile, Iranian-Western

---

happened. The USSR intervened militarily while the United States supported the Afghan fighting forces.

relations deteriorated. The British and Americans desperately sought to negotiate a compromise with the Iranian government, which, despite the internal societal upheavals brought about by these events, displayed an unwavering firmness that led to the severing of diplomatic relations with Britain on October 22, 1952, under the leadership of Prime Minister Mohammad Mossadegh. A few months later, Operation Ajax took shape. Combining British (MI6) and American intelligence services (CIA), a decision validated by Prime Minister Winston Churchill (who returned to office in October 1951), and President Dwight Eisenhower aimed to overthrow Mohammad Mossadegh, who was thought to be planning to sell Iranian oil to the USSR. In August 1953, the country was plunged into great uncertainty when the Shah fled, and Operation Ajax failed to topple the Prime Minister... at first. This tumultuous situation lasted only a few days. In great secrecy, the CIA met with General Fazlollah Zahedi, who had once supported Mohammad Mossadegh's party, but who had since distanced himself from the latter. On August 19, the military officer finally gained the upper hand over the Prime Minister, not without difficulty. The Shah was then able to return to Tehran.

I have deliberately chosen not to go into the details of Operation Ajax and to give only a summary of it because the result shows that, despite the interventions of foreign intelligence services, the Shah never went back on the nationalization of the oil industry in his country. However, he did negotiate an agreement with several Western companies, including those already present. There is a proverb that says, "to make the best of a bad situation." This spirit animated the Iranian-Western negotiations. London and Washington succeeded: Tehran did not have to get any closer to Moscow. As for Iran, the nationalization of its oil industry gave ideas to others who also sought to be able to exploit and profit from their natural resources... and to no longer be subject to any form of foreign domination. Worse, Shah Mohammad Reza Pahlavi himself was instrumental in creating a new troublemaker in international relations: OPEC.

In September 1960, Saudi Arabia, Iraq, Iran, Kuwait, and Venezuela founded the famous oil cartel in Baghdad. The Cold War was still raging. Shortly after OPEC was set up, the world was plunged into anxiety with the Berlin crisis, which lasted for several years, but above all with the Cuban missile affair, which almost degenerated into a nuclear conflict. In the meantime, Moscow was jubilant after successfully sending the first man into space. This event prompted President John Fitzgerald Kennedy to launch the United States into an unprecedented space program: to conquer the Moon during the current decade. The technological confrontation started again. Among the events of the moment, I would like to add an event that took place on October 27, 1962, and the mysterious disappearance of Enrico Mattei in a plane crash, the all-powerful boss of ENI, the great Italian hydrocarbon company that he built into a veritable state within a state. He died under murky circumstances that have never been clarified since. Several hypotheses emerged without ever providing irrefutable proof. However, some of them led to a vendetta operated by Western powers within the framework of the Cold War and the decolonization process in North Africa. The sixties were thus more uncertain than ever. To this particularly anxious climate, one had to consider decolonization and the wars of independence that sometimes punctuated the break with the former colonial power. In other words, the creation of OPEC did not come at any time. In fact, the organization developed rapidly to the point of becoming a major player in international relations within a decade, one of those capable of worrying both the White House and the Kremlin, of disturbing and upsetting the East-West rivalry. The cartel was not to be trifled with! The oil producers understood that they had considerable leverage in attacking production, supplies, and exchange prices. From the 1970s onwards, the consumption of black gold exploded worldwide. Faced with a rapidly growing demand, oil became the pressure tactic par excellence. This trend is still confirmed today, despite the discourse advocating a decarbonization of the world economy.

In the early 1970s, Europe began to show signs of economic decline. Its oil needs were increasing, and it was dependent on hydrocarbon imports, mainly from the Middle East. The end of the famous *"Trente Glorieuses"* was inexorably approaching. Within the Western alliance, still during the Cold War, a process of European economic construction was launched, formalized by the signing of the Treaties of Rome in 1957. [23] Within NATO, the tone was different. France, under the presidency of Charles de Gaulle, withdrew from the integrated command of the organization in 1966. This decision sounded like a real thunderclap. The man of the Liberation motivated this decision by exposing his desire to see France regain its full sovereignty over its territory and pointed the finger at the strong American military presence within it. As a reminder, France had experienced a bitter debacle in Indochina a decade earlier and was emerging from the painful war in Algeria. It had no choice but to resolve to lose its colonial empire. Charles de Gaulle was wary of an imposing foreign

---

[23] Author's note: In 1951, France, Germany, Italy and the three Benelux countries signed an agreement on coal and steel, the famous ECSC Treaty for European Coal and Steel Community. In 1957, these same countries embarked on a process of further collaboration as the Treaties of Rome established the European Economic Community (EEC) and the European Atomic Energy Community (EAEC), also known as Euratom.

military presence on his territory. It was important to him that France not fall under the yoke of the United States. This diplomatic crisis never called into question the idea of a Western alliance against the Communist bloc. The whole camp was generally pulling in the same direction... which caused a few oil-related inconveniences.

Between 1970 and 1973, the selling price of black gold doubled. It did not exceed a few US dollars, but in view of the sharply rising volumes of imports, this increased the energy bill of buyers. On October 6, 1973, the Yom Kippur War broke out. It pitted the State of Israel against Egypt and Syria. The two Arab countries had attacked the territories occupied by the Hebrew state since the Six-Day War, helped by the support of several other Arab powers, some of which were Islamic in culture, and others communist. [24] The Israeli response was not long in coming. In less than three weeks, Jerusalem won a military victory. The outcome of the war had an impact on Israel's allies. Indeed, the Persian Gulf oil producing countries decided to sanction them by reducing their production. This immediately led to a shortage of supply available on the market. Trading prices soared and quadrupled in the space of a few weeks. Worse, Saudi Arabia imposed an embargo on exports to the United States. A wind of panic blew over the Western world. Economic growth slowed sharply, and unemployment rose alarmingly. The oil crisis came to an end in 1974 when Israel's allies shifted their diplomatic support to Jerusalem.

The 1973 shock was the peak of OPEC's influence in international relations. The organization has seen its importance decline over time, although its power of

---

[24] Author's note: At the end of the Six-Day War in June 1967, the State of Israel occupied territories taken from Syria in the Golan Heights and from Egypt in the Sinai Peninsula.

influence should not be underestimated. What I call decline corresponds to the fact that the shock of 1973 acted in its time as an electroshock on the buyers of black gold. They realized that they had to find ways to reduce their dependence on this natural resource, especially for electricity production. For this reason, France began to build nuclear power plants. Italy and the United Kingdom opted for natural gas, while West Germany chose to diversify its electricity production through coal, nuclear and natural gas. But it took more than that to keep oil off the international agenda!

A trauma that has been experienced implies its share of lessons to be learned, but it never provides immunity against a phenomenon of the bis repetita type. The wake-up call orchestrated by OPEC in 1973 did nothing to solve the world's oil problems. Although the market eased from 1974 onwards, it plummeted again in 1979, a pivotal year marked by a succession of events that had a heavy impact on the oil sector. The Islamic Revolution swept away the last hopes of the Shah of Iran, who resolved to end his days in exile. A few months later, tensions between Tehran and Washington rose with the hostage-taking at the American embassy in the Iranian capital. This affair changed forever the American diplomatic position in the Middle East. In December 1979, Soviet troops entered Afghanistan and embarked on an armed conflict that lasted for a decade. All these events contributed to an increasingly uncertain future for the world. The following year, a fierce war broke out between Iran and Iraq. The armed opposition lasted eight years and led to the stopping of Iranian oil exports...

To summarize the situation succinctly, within a few months, there was a major political change in Iran that strained the geopolitical climate in the Middle East. Second, two major oil producers and members of OPEC engaged in a deadly and destructive conflict, which caused a significant drop in world production of this commodity. Third, the two opposing Cold War superpowers were involved in major crises in Asia, the United States in Iran, and the USSR in Afghanistan. This was beginning to have a major impact on the oil market, which saw its exchange prices almost triple between 1978 and 1981. The economic consequences were worldwide, and undoubtedly more severe than those caused by the 1973 oil shock. The surge in prices slowed down the economic development of many countries that had gained independence a few years earlier and were struggling to find domestic socio-political stability. It had an impact on the Asian dragons, which were then experiencing very dynamic economic growth requiring ever greater needs for black gold. Japan's main oil partner was Iran. As for the Western world, the economic boom of the *"Trente Glorieuses"* had already been over for several years. Oil was expensive for its importers and the Cold War was entering a decisive phase. The world's great game was on fire for good. Ronald Reagan won the race for the White House in 1980, while 1982 marked the end of the Brezhnev era in the USSR on November 10. The duel of the superpowers would soon deliver its verdict.

Considering the ongoing crises mentioned above, the arrival of Mikhail Gorbachev in the cockpit of the sinking USSR did not help. He succeeded Konstantin Chernenko in March 1985, but his *glasnost* and *perestroika* reforms [25] came too late in a dying national economy. The nation's future looked difficult, but no one expected the two crushing blows of 1986 that precipitated Moscow and the Communist bloc to the collapse of the system. Firstly, on the night of April 25-26, the Kremlin learned of a nuclear incident in the Ukrainian Soviet. It tried to conceal the

---

[25] Author's note: *Glasnost* translates as transparency; *perestroika* as reconstruction.

information and minimize its importance... before understanding the gravity of the situation. The Chernobyl disaster left a lasting impression on the world, but in the context of the Cold War, it revealed the USSR's inability to deal with this type of problem and the gaping holes in its faltering system. Secondly, another event severely affected Soviet finances a few weeks after Chernobyl: the oil counter-shock of 1986. In an international context of economic recession, an agreement between the United States and Saudi Arabia on production influenced exchange prices downwards. While the Iraq-Iran war was still raging, Washington's Western allies saw their oil needs increase. The solution was therefore to boost production, which Riyadh agreed to meet. The Wahhabi kingdom did not shy away from the opportunity to increase its revenues assured by its growing production and this despite the drop in exchange prices in the making. On the other hand, for the USSR, this new deal was like a death sentence. Part of the Soviet income came from the sale of hydrocarbons and this configuration augured disastrous consequences for the national economy... and that of the satellite states, which suffered from the cuts in aid provided by the Kremlin. The edifice was inexorably cracking. The old decoy techniques aimed at impressing the West no longer worked. The USSR lacked everything and could no longer help its sister countries. As a symbol, an attempt was made to celebrate the 40th anniversary of the German Democratic Republic (GDR) in October 1989. Most of the leaders of the communist states came to Berlin, including Mikhail Gorbachev. The East German people rumbled and invaded the streets of East Berlin. As for the heads of state present, they all understood that the end was near. In fact, the local leader Erich Honecker, who was admittedly ill, resigned a few days later. As for the big Soviet brother, it watched, powerless and dying, as the communist era came to an end in East Germany. The celebration in Berlin was in name only. No one had the heart to celebrate. History was already in motion. A month later, the Wall of Shame fell. A domino effect followed. The USSR was living its last months of existence, while Germany reunified between 1990 and 1991, leaving communist rule behind forever. *Good Bye Lenin!* [26]

It is important to remember that oil was not the only factor in the collapse of the communist bloc, but it did contribute actively. To give an idea of the weight of hydrocarbons in the Soviet economy, oil production increased by more than 70% between the seventies and eighties. [27] As for gas production, it broke all records since it had a multiplier coefficient of two hundred and six [28] between 1945 and 1990. These statistics show the extent to which the USSR expected to generate increasing revenues through the export of its natural resources, including black gold. This frenetic quest to increase hydrocarbon production reflects the need to generate ever-increasing revenues due to the economic needs of the struggle against the Western bloc. The difficulty (or risk) lays in the fact that by increasing production in such proportions, the USSR was exposed to provoke an imbalance in supply and demand if the latter did not follow. In the case of oil, this scenario

---

[26] Author's note: This is a reference to the film directed by Wolfgang Becker (2003). The story is about a family in East Berlin and its matriarch who was very involved in the social life of this communist regime. During the celebration of the fortieth anniversary of the GDR, this woman suffered a health problem that plunged her into a coma that lasted several months. When she woke up, the Wall had already fallen, but her relatives, fearing her reaction to the end of the communist era, opted for an atypical choice: to hide the truth from her at all costs by trying to recreate a bygone era.

[27] Stéphane Dubois, *"La Russie et ses hydrocarbures : la tactique à court terme aux dépens de la stratégie à long terme ?," Géoéconomie 2009/1 n°48,* pp. 67 to 88

[28] *Ibid.*

occurred with the combined aggressive policy of Saudi Arabia and Kuwait on black gold production. World supply outstripped demand and trading prices collapsed, much to the chagrin of the USSR still reeling from the Chernobyl disaster. The colossus with feet of clay fell to its knees and never rose again. Thus ended the Cold War. And so began a new era of international relations, that of the affirmation of a dominant superpower in the world: the United States of America. Once again, black gold played a leading role.

The new post-Cold War world order

When the Wall of Shame fell in Berlin on November 9, 1989, it symbolized the end of a four-decade long era: the Cold War. Unlike wars, which are characterized by loss of life and material destruction, none of this happened in the East-West conflict, but the big loser emerged weakened to the point of breaking up forever sometime later. The end of the Soviet period was looming dangerously large in Moscow. Wars of independence definitively destroyed the last hopes of keeping intact a union of soviets in name only. In the satellite states of Central and Eastern Europe, people also chose to break free from the yoke of the Kremlin and to rediscover a sense of freedom, sometimes at a high price. In Romania, the leader Nicolae Ceausescu and his wife were executed on Christmas Day 1989 after an expeditious trial like those that characterized justice under communist rule. The country thus marked its desire to open a new chapter in its history and to detach itself from the influence of Moscow. Above all, the countries of Central and Eastern Europe needed to recover economically and ensure a smooth transition to new political governance. Less than fifteen years later, several of them joined the European Union (EU) as it expanded eastward.

The USSR never recovered from the accumulation of bad news in the 1980s. Since the destruction of the Berlin Wall, the giant with the hammer and sickle continued its long agony until its total disappearance in 1991. From this came fifteen new independent states [29] which would later thwart the designs of oil geopolitics. As for Russia, Boris Yeltsin succeeded Mikhail Gorbachev, who was ordered to step down from his leadership position. The country's

---

[29] Author's note: Russia, Latvia, Lithuania, Estonia, Belarus, Ukraine, Moldova, Georgia, Armenia, Azerbaijan, Kazakhstan, Uzbekistan, Kyrgyzstan, Tajikistan, and Turkmenistan.

economy was bloodless. Many imagined that Moscow would sink into a long-lasting socio-economic crisis. In any case, the Russian capital no longer worried the Western camp, and more particularly the United States, which emerged victorious from this bitter ideological confrontation.

In Washington, a sweet aroma of unparalleled power spread through the nation's political and economic leadership. With the collapse of the USSR, one witnessed the consecration of an era without equivalent in modern history, since never had a state dominated the world as much as the United States at the end of the Cold War. No one disputed this hegemonic domination of the economy, diplomacy, culture, and other areas in which it sometimes seemed as if the planet was split in two, the United States on one side and the rest of the world on the other. And America's military power far surpassed that of any other nation. This unprecedented situation stimulated the thinking of many political scientists. Several theses became landmarks. Francis Fukuyama published *The End of History and the Last Man* [30] , a major work in which he set out the vision that democracy and liberalism would always triumph in the end over any other system of governance. Samuel Huntington, on the other hand, did not share this view and believed that no system was immune to the return of an ideology. In this intellectual battle, it turned out that the end of the war offered a previously unknown scenario that was therefore difficult to analyze. Some imagined that the American reign would be long and radiant.

Three decades later, the post-Cold War ultra-domination is no more. On the other hand, oil has always been at the heart of the considerations of power games,

---

[30] Francis Fukuyama, *The End of History and the Last Man*, Free Press, 1992, 418 p.

especially in view of the emergence of China and its necessity to satisfy its oil needs to ensure its economic growth. In the same way, black gold occupied a central place in the international relations of the early 1990s. In the introductory part of this book, I briefly mentioned the first Gulf War. When I mention this region, I must mention Hormuz, the name of the strait through which most of the world's oil traffic passes. The control of strategic passages and major maritime routes of black gold has been growing in importance in the priorities of the main dominant powers ever since. Oil vindicates Sir Walter Raleigh's 1600 postulate that *"for whosoever commands the sea commands the trade; whosoever commands the trade of the world commands the riches of the world, and consequently the world itself."*

When one looks at the evolution of international relations since the end of the Cold War, several trends related to oil are becoming more and more evident. Global demand for oil continues to grow. National economies, the less advanced, emerging, and established ones, require ever more consistent and secure supplies. International relations seem to be as uncertain and tense as ever in oil-producing areas or sensitive oil transit points. Other factors have contributed to make black gold an increasingly coveted element... and a source of anxiety as soon as something leaves a doubt or a threat around this precious natural resource. Just look at the emotion generated on the financial markets as soon as there is any worrying news about black gold. They immediately go into overdrive! A resurgence of tension relating to Iran, whatever its origin, and the prospect of a disruption of traffic in the Strait of Hormuz soon spread waves of anxiety among all those who buy from producers in the region.

In the previous chapter, I sought to show the complexity of international relations in the 1980s. Among the major crises mentioned, the war between Iraq and Iran lasted for eight years and probably took the lives of more than a million people. It is important to remember that Baghdad received financial support from the Arab monarchies of the Persian Gulf, as well as logistical support from the Western world. The oil-monarchies did not like the regime change in Iran in 1979, a country with a Shiite majority, while the latter are essentially Sunni. At the end of the war, Iraq and Iran could only see the damage, considering the economic impact of the drop in oil exports, the main source of income for both countries. At the same time, the USSR was preparing to leave the Afghan hell, defeated, and bruised by this military failure. Within the Eastern bloc, Moscow's influence had definitively lost its superbness. The world was moving, and Saddam Hussein asked his two main financiers, Saudi Arabia, and Kuwait, to write off his debts... but they refused. This reaction provoked the anger of the Iraqi Rais. After analyzing the situation, the Berlin Wall falling in the meantime and confirming the end of the Cold War, he undertook to "compensate" by invading the Kuwaiti territory and taking advantage of the uncertainty that had fallen on international relations with the collapse of the Communist bloc and the upcoming breakup of the USSR.

The Iraqi leader voiced several grievances against Saudi Arabia and Kuwait, in addition to the fact that they did not want to cancel their debts. He blamed the small emirate for not respecting production quotas as defined by OPEC, which had a downward impact on exchange prices. Baghdad then argued for a higher selling price per barrel to generate more revenue. On the other hand, Saddam Hussein did not accept that his two Arab neighbors had taken advantage of the Iran-Iraq war and their declining production of black gold to increase theirs, conquer market share and pocket very lucrative profits. The Iraqi loss of revenue was in the billions of US dollars and heavily penalized the national economy while the Wahhabi kingdom and the neighboring emirate became richer. Other grievances were added to this growing resentment, which led to irreparability. Despite several attempts at dialogue to appease his anger, Saddam Hussein invaded Kuwait on August 2, 1990, claiming that the emirate had once been part of the Ottoman entity of Basra. [31] At the international level, there was an immediate reaction condemning the hostile attitude of the Iraqi leader. On the same day, the UN Security Council passed resolution 600. This text condemned the invasive operation, demanded the withdrawal of Iraqi troops from Kuwaiti territory and urged the two countries concerned to engage in peace negotiations. At the same time, economic sanctions were imposed on Iraq.

In this turbulent post-Cold War context, Baghdad did not comply with the injunctions of resolution 600. On November 29, 1990, the Security Council passed resolution 678, which authorized the use of force against the Iraqi armies if they had not left Kuwaiti territory by January 15, 1991. Saddam Hussein maintained his position. He had not yet understood it, but a new world order was taking shape. Indeed, the collapse of the USSR and its alliance with the communist satellite states profoundly changed the international relations of the time since only one superpower survived the Cold War, the United States. Since November 1989, the strong man in Washington was George H. W. Bush, a personality with a remarkable career. He used to be Ronald Reagan's Vice-President for eight years,

---

[31] Author's note: Independent since 1961, Kuwait had already been the subject of claims from Baghdad in the late 1950s and at the time of independence.

but previously served as Director of the CIA and as his country's Ambassador to the United Nations. His pedigree as a former diplomat and director of the world's largest intelligence agency complemented that of a statesman otherwise influenced by the neo-conservatives, the same ones who advised his son, George W. Bush, a decade later and played a significant role in the second war in Iraq starting in 2003. With the Iraqi invasion of Kuwait, George Bush understood above all that he had to make history, the history that corresponded to the new chapter in international relations of the 1990s.

To avoid any confusion, I would like to remind you that the first Gulf War occurred because of Iraqi aggression against its neighbor Kuwait and that the military operation led by an international coalition was legitimized by the United Nations. The United States took a leading role in this conflict. It deployed considerable human and logistical resources to crush the Iraqi troops. It was a question of revealing to the world its striking force and showing to anyone its military superpower. The invasion of Kuwait, on the other hand, led to unprecedented propaganda and lies against Iraq. The Iraqi army was presented as "the fourth most powerful in the world." The aim was to give an even more dramatic dimension to the threat posed by Iraq. It turned out that the Iraqi army was not that powerful. Also, in the weeks before the vote on resolution 678, a Kuwaiti nurse testified before the U.S. Congress to denounce the horrors committed by the Iraqis in her country. It was later discovered that this testimony was a lie and that its sole purpose was to stir up international public opinion and support military intervention against Saddam Hussein's armies... This lie is strangely reminiscent of the one about the weapons of mass destruction allegedly held by the Iraqi regime in the 2000s...

My reflection does not focus on the lies of history, but on the geopolitical impact of the first Gulf War. The international coalition led by the United States defeated Iraq. Beyond the military aspect, Washington sent a message to the international community that anyone who stepped out of line would face American wrath. Saddam Hussein retained his leadership of Iraq, but he had lost big. As for the oil stakes, this armed intervention favored Saudi Arabia and the other Arab producers in the region, who thus benefited from the banning of Iraq and Iran. This situation therefore weakened OPEC on the international scene because of the quarrels between several of its members. However, the military intervention in Kuwait also had unexpected consequences in the Arabian Peninsula. King Fahd of Saudi Arabia allowed the United States to establish military bases in the Wahhabi kingdom. [32] The decision sparked waves of protest in the country. Moreover, if the United States bought some of its imported oil from Saudi Arabia, Washington feared that the regime would be destabilized, a fear that was further confirmed when the ruler suffered a stroke in 1995, an incident that caused much discord within the ruling family regarding the succession. In other words, Riyadh was going through a complicated and uncertain period. For Washington, if a severe crisis were to break out in Saudi Arabia and hypothetically disrupt oil supplies, it was important to find other suppliers. Iraq became an option to consider, despite the sanctions on its oil export limitations. In 2001, Washington was buying nearly 800,000 barrels per day from Baghdad, making it its sixth largest supplier of black gold. [33] That same year, on

---

[32] Author's note: This American military presence had several advantages in Washington's eyes. A permanent human presence made it possible to have observation posts near enemy states, Iraq, and Iran in this case. It also contributed to the development of Washington's desired foreign policy in the Middle East as well as to the defense of American economic interests in the region.

January 20, George W. Bush took up residence at 1600 Pennsylvania Avenue. Iraq was once again in the crosshairs of the United States, this time for the wrong reasons. In the presidential entourage, there were certain personalities already linked to the oil world. By planning to remove Saddam Hussein from power for good, it was imagined that the future leadership team would favor American industry... All that was needed was to find the right context to justify a new muscular intervention on Iraqi soil. With the weapons of mass destruction, the White House and its surrounding hawks intended to put an end to the dictator's reign.

I now go back and briefly summarize the international situation at the end of the first Gulf War. The American domination through its hard and soft powers appeared to be striking. The USSR was living its last hours. In Europe, the EEC was about to become the EU in 1992 after the signing of the Maastricht Treaty. However, the Old Continent could not compete with the political, economic, and military power of its American ally. Elsewhere, two demographic giants still impressed no one in the West. China and India were gradually emerging. In the Middle Kingdom, economic growth was dynamic, but for many analysts, the country had a long way to go, and this growth dynamic would sooner or later reach its limits. In Eastern Europe, the USSR had finally broken up into new independent states. The new Russia was a sight to behold. Its convalescence was likely to be long. This is how one thought in 1992-1993.

In my opinion, there was a major event at the dawn of the third millennium: the attacks of September 11, 2001. The Western world then realized that a new enemy had appeared and that it would have to fight a new kind of

---

[33] Olivier Da Lage, *"Une guerre pour le pétrole ? Pas seulement, mais...,"* Outre-Terre, 2003/4 n°5, pp. 95 to 113

terrorism. In 2001, Vladimir Putin was already President of Russia. People started to talk about extremely wealthy Russian citizens who were referred to as oligarchs. They had built their fortune on the ruins of the defunct USSR. They had benefited from the privatization policies implemented under Mikhail Gorbachev from 1988 onwards and then by Boris Yeltsin, particularly in the sectors exploiting natural resources, including oil. The Russian economy owes its revival mainly to the gradual rise in the exchange prices of raw materials. The first decade of the new millennium saw Russia's return to the international scene in a big way. Between 1998 and 2008, the selling price of OPEC crude oil rose from an average of $12.28 to $94.1. [34] Until his legal troubles in 2003, the richest man in Russia was Mikhail Khodorkovsky. He ran the Russian oil giant Yukos. In 2003, his group was to sell most of its shares to the American groups ExxonMobil and Chevron Texaco. The operation failed. In Moscow, the takeover of the national oil giant by American investors was certainly not looked upon favorably. In the meantime, Russia no longer looked like a dying giant after the Cold War.

Also in 2001, China was no longer perceived as an emerging power but rather as a giant in the making, and even as the country that would eventually challenge American leadership. Beijing had changed dimension in less than a decade. Until the mid-1990s, the country was self-sufficient in oil, but its need for black gold grew considerably as its economy developed. Clearly, oil was one of the engines of its economic growth. For China, it was now necessary to find suppliers and above all to secure supplies. When the Bush Administration took over the reins of American governance, Beijing was already no longer a laughingstock in Washington. It was important to thwart the

---

[34] *"Prix annuel moyen du pétrole brut de l'OPEP entre 1960 et 2022,"* fr.statista.com, February 3, 2023

Middle Kingdom's oil supplies. This meant that the United States had to rethink its foreign policy in the Middle East and Central Asia, especially in the former Soviet republics. The rise of China's economic power was probably a factor considered by the Bush Administration in view of a new military intervention in Iraq. The destruction of the country led to a reconstruction for which the most influential spheres in Washington expected to win lucrative contracts. Considering Iraq's oil reserves and China's growing needs, they were eager to convince the future ruling elites not to sell the precious sesame to the Asian giant. With time, it turned out that China managed to negotiate delivery contracts with Saudi Arabia, Iraq, and Iran.

American foreign policy in the Middle East and Central Asia deserves some reflection. First, while the military intervention in Afghanistan was justified considering the September 2001 attacks and its sponsors sheltered by the Taliban regime, the war in Iraq was based on a blatant lie that concealed unavoidable intentions. The American presence in these two countries has certainly contributed to the rise of anti-Americanism in many jurisdictions of Islamic culture. Second, since Xi Jinping came to power in China, the world's second largest economy has made no secret of its ambitions. It hopes to conquer the leadership of the world economy. It is giving itself the means to do so. The huge infrastructure project to restore the Silk Roads illustrates China's desire to develop its commercial networks on a large scale. Before the Xi Jinping era, the Middle Kingdom already possessed substantial means to satisfy its commercial diplomacy and its domestic needs, particularly in terms of energy. China wanted to be more discreet, but it advanced its pawns patiently, according to its interests. In Central Asia, it circumvented the designs of Washington's neo-conservative hawks by investing massively in infrastructure projects that already foreshadowed the new Silk Roads policy. In countries that were once Soviet and in which Russia has always sought to retain influence since their independence, China has deployed subtle and effective diplomacy to secure supplies of oil and gas... in geographic areas where the United States can hardly thwart Chinese plans. Third, in the same vein, Beijing is working to shift the center of gravity of the global economy to the East. This also applies to oil. The best way to secure supplies of black gold is to reduce transport distances as much as possible and to avoid transiting through sensitive crossing points such as the Strait of Malacca, which is subject to security problems. This objective is part of the motivations linked to the new Silk Roads. Nevertheless, considering the tensions between Russia and the Western world, one understands that the sanctions enacted regarding the war in Ukraine had been anticipated by Moscow since the crisis of 2014 and the war in Donbass which started in April. The following month, a giant contract in the gas sector sealed an agreement between the Chinese CNPC and the Russian Gazprom. Of course, it was about gas instead of oil. But the important message was that Russia was looking to the Eastern world. It saw China as a partner that could provide it with large volumes of hydrocarbon purchases. As the two Eurasian giants share common borders, Beijing saw the double advantage of securing supplies of fossil fuels while positioning itself on large volumes to be imported. You get the point: China buys a lot of oil from its Russian neighbor. The war in Ukraine has greatly contributed to strengthening this trade. Russia has become China's leading supplier, and China has been the world's largest importer of black gold for several years.

Since the advent of the American hyperpower, a designation immortalized in France by the former head of diplomacy Hubert Védrine [35], oil has had a constant influence on international relations. At a time when the scientific world is urging public decision-makers to promote the public policies needed to decarbonize the world economy, it seems to me that the oil sector has a bright future ahead of it. When an alarm is sounded, the recipients of the message agree and say they have heard the message. Everything becomes more complicated when it is a question of acting and above all of countering economic, political, strategic, or other interests that are de facto more important than the evils denounced. Since the Earth Summit held in Rio de Janeiro in 1992, oil consumption has never stopped growing in the world. Once again, the more one denounces, the more one consumes. I am not pointing the finger of blame; the world is suffering from a disease that the medical world calls addiction. To cure a patient, it is necessary to administer the right remedy. Still, it is necessary that he deigns to consume it.

The official discourse, the one that drives the annual UN climate conferences, points the finger at fossil fuels. One consumes too much of them. They contribute to global warming. It is becoming urgent to act and to obtain significant results. One keeps on doing it every year... while the scientific studies conducted by the IPCC regularly announce more and more worrying results. When it comes to oil, one is taking a very cautious approach. Basically, it continues to be a major factor in international relations, financial markets, and the global economy. As with alcohol or tobacco, prevention campaigns are promoted to denounce the risks associated with their over-consumption. The same is done with the excessive use of black gold and its by-products, but one is not letting up despite the good will of those who wish to embark on the path of decarbonization as the EU is promoting so much. For many reasons, some

---

[35] Hubert Védrine, *Face à l'hyper-puissance. Textes et discours 1995-2003*, Fayard, September 2003, 384 p.

cannot reduce their dependence while others do not want to. How many national economies are based on economic growth performance linked to the satisfaction of growing oil needs? As for the leverage that this natural resource provides, it goes without saying that it drives many international intrigues. If I refer to OPEC, for example, its influence has declined in international relations, especially since the end of the Cold War, but not that of oil. The actors change and evolve but black gold retains its central importance in the major global issues. For it, one continues to kill and betray without scruples. One reconciles based on oil issues. Lethal weapon for some and miracle cure for others, it is above all indispensable. The world has revolved around it for more than a century. The last few years will not contradict this impression.

Black gold still at the heart of major maneuvers

In December 2015, the world's press reported news that was to have a major impact on the course of international relations. However, at the time of the announcement, few understood the true significance of what was afoot: the United States was about to lift an old ban on the export of domestically produced oil. Within months, the world oil market went into a tailspin as trading prices continued to fall over the previous year. Washington had given its approval to American producers to flood the world with its black gold. With this significant increase in supply, prices fell. This was to the detriment of many producers who were slow to understand and react to stop the hemorrhage, as the massive influx of American oil seriously upset the economic models of many countries, especially those that relied on their oil rents.

However, it seems to me that a little background is in order. Barack Obama was entering his last year in office. The Constitution of his country did not allow him to run for a third consecutive term, so he had to give way to someone else. Donald Trump had already announced his intention to run in the Republican primary. When I mention December 2015, I must recall that COP 21 had just ended and the Paris Climate Agreement, a text ardently defended by Barack Obama, had punctuated a climactic finale for an event that had long feared a frustrating conclusion devoid of a comprehensive agreement. At the end of the event, the hard-negotiated text was hailed as a step towards committing the international community to public policies aimed at combating climate change. In the dock, hydrocarbons were facing their detractors. I was about to leave out another point: the tensions between Russia and Ukraine due to the Russian annexation of Crimea the previous year and the fighting that has plagued the Donbass region since then. Already.

I will not venture to denounce any form of disguised hypocrisy, but the United States has admirably leveraged its commitment to climate change to better defend its oil interests and boost its leverage in international relations. Barack Obama advocated for public policies committed to the fight against global warming and promoted renewable energy. He undoubtedly committed himself to this path. At the same time, he had to avoid upsetting the powerful oil lobby, which was beginning to fear these new energy policies. It was therefore important to find common ground. The compromise had to be based on giving oil companies the opportunity to produce black gold and export it to international markets. Since the 1970s and the first oil crisis, the black gold produced in the United States had been intended for domestic consumption. President Obama was thus making a considerable change of course, which quickly became a political and economic success for its designers.

It was a political success because by promoting renewable energy and offering U.S. oil producers the opportunity to export, President Obama was able to set himself up as a strong advocate for the fight against climate change because the United States was committed to leading by example. But no one was communicating about allowing domestic oil producers to increase production for economic purposes. Washington's interest was in demonstrating a strong commitment to effective action on climate change.

The big oil players got away with selling their abundant production... and contributing to the increase in supply on the world market. By flooding the market, supply outstripped demand. Trading prices immediately fell. The strength of US-made oil was based on the exploitation of shale deposits. These shale deposits had the particularity of offering their operators an exceptionally high profitability compared to so-called conventional deposits. For this reason, it is important to understand that a shale deposit does not require as much investment as a conventional deposit and that it can be exploited in a much shorter period. In other words, a U.S. shale oil producer operates with comfortable margins while offering a lower selling price than its international competitors. Considering that the United States has substantial reserves of this oily treasure, the opportunity was obviously too good to pass up. The oil pump was thus activated to destabilize the two other major world producers: Russia and Saudi Arabia. In both cases, a significant and lasting drop in the price of black gold would be detrimental, since both countries base a large part of their national economic model on the sale of hydrocarbons. Such a prospect did not displease Washington. As a reminder, President Obama maintained cool relations with Russia, while the loyal Saudi ally was dismayed by his willingness to re-establish dialogue with Iran to find a diplomatic solution to the nuclear issue. Washington-Riyadh relations became strained. The Wahhabi kingdom thus did not take a dim view of Donald Trump's victory in November 2016. A few months later, the latter made his first state visit by going to Saudi Arabia, anything but a coincidence.

The year 2016 saw oil trading prices fall without a break. The trend, which began in 2014, was confirmed more than ever in a global climate of market misunderstanding and lying poker. Meanwhile, the Russians and the Saudis were wondering. What was to be done? The logic of the moment was to reduce supply to raise exchange prices. Such an option naturally favored American producers who were only too happy to conquer international market share. A major question hovered: was the economic model of shale oil viable? Moscow and Riyadh took the view that the United States could not maintain such a level of production indefinitely and that trading prices would eventually rise. A few years later, it turned out that everyone was wrong about shale oil... except the United States, which continued its production policy. In short, despite the drop in exchange prices, American producers made large profits because of the margins they made and the volumes they sold. For Russia and Saudi Arabia, the trend of the moment alerted their leaders. The conclusion was clear: the United States was not bluffing. Worse, it was taking advantage of the situation while the Russian and Saudi national economies were feeling the effects of lower trading prices more and more.

When the Trump tornado triumphed in the November 2016 presidential election, it quickly confirmed some campaign promises, particularly around climate change. Donald Trump set out to withdraw the United States from the Paris Climate Agreement. For many, he had just torpedoed the international community's efforts to make a real energy transition. The whimsical new American strongman doubted the climate change thesis. Above all, he was counting on a competitive oil sector. If his country was to establish itself as the world's great oil power, he intended to strengthen the political and economic leadership of the United States. To do this, he had to act on oil. By supporting a policy of lowering the price of black gold, he was not content with thwarting the economic plans of Russia and Saudi Arabia, with whom he hoped to change diplomatic course. Another political and economic power in the sights of Donald Trump was more worrying: China. The latter needed to secure its oil supplies in view of its growing domestic needs. It was therefore necessary to insist on this weak point and to allow American producers to be ever more influential on international markets.

By all appearances, Donald Trump had undertaken a work of deconstruction or demolition of the diplomatic and energy initiatives implemented by his predecessor. There is some truth to this statement, but it must be qualified. While he did not share Barack Obama's vision on climate change, the two men came to a common conclusion regarding the oil sector: it was necessary to satisfy its players and boost their economic activity for eminently strategic reasons. From then on, regardless of the political leanings of the strongman in the White House, these industrialists had the assurance of seeing their business prosper internationally. Thus, American political decision-makers and oil companies found a common ground that suited everyone. Each was indeed defending its own interests, but by opting for such a strategy, they were converging. Once again, this scenario worked perfectly, as few believed in the viability of the shale oil business model.

The United States benefited from an exceptional alignment of the planets. They were able to take advantage of a global climate of uncertainty in which the Russians and the Saudis refused to intervene in any way regarding production. Indeed, the first to intervene in this sense ran the risk of being perceived as being in economic difficulty; yet in international relations, no one openly exposes their difficulties. However, no one was fooled. Russia and Saudi Arabia had no interest in seeing trading prices fall continuously without reacting. Their economic health was at stake. No one took the lead and prices continued to fall. The United States was gloating. American oil was flowing around the world while its main competitors blamed each other for being the first to draw on production policies... This situation showed the complexity of the interconnections of geopolitical and geostrategic interests. When I refer to a situation of liar's poker, I cannot think of a better image to describe this situation, this tug-of-war that opposed Moscow and Riyadh for months, each one waiting for the other to resolve to put an end to this vertiginous fall in crude oil trading prices by reducing its production. At the same time, both believed that the current U.S. strategy of flooding the world with black gold would not be sustainable, in other words, that the United States was playing a bluff for a limited time. And yet, it took advantage of this windfall. Washington continued to torpedo the market price by running the oil pump at full speed.

I express my opinions in all transparency. At the time of the events, I was one of the numerous analysts who did not believe in the viability of the American model based on the exploitation of shale oil. At the time, I was not familiar with this economic model, which was very different from that of conventional oil, but I was basing myself on a rational argument: by acting in this way, the United States found itself isolated on the world oil market, since its objectives were fundamentally different from those of the other producers. Although it accounted for nearly 15% of world production, it remained a minority in the market and exposed itself to a coalition wishing to act against the fall in exchange prices... which only came about very late, when the bleeding had to be stopped.

The "watering can" scenario became clearer for Washington when an unexpected and extremely damaging event occurred in 2020: the Covid-19 health crisis. This resulted in a considerable drop in world demand for black gold, while supply remained overabundant. Trading prices immediately plummeted to the point of being catastrophic for American producers. The White House and Donald Trump urgently needed to intervene, inviting their Russian and Saudi competitors to dialogue to resolve the crisis. In April 2020, the U.S. markets collapsed to the point of offering negative exchange prices. In other words, stockholders had to pay buyers to get rid of their raw materials... In the run-up to the health crisis, the state of the market benefited Donald Trump as the strongman of the U.S. executive branch engaged in the most aggressive diplomacy with his traditional allies. To fulfill his campaign promises, particularly regarding the famous slogan *Make America great again*, he ventured out on his own on the international scene. He isolated himself from the Western world, re-established more courteous relations with Russia and Vladimir Putin, restored privileged ties with Saudi Arabia and, above all, designated China as the United States' main enemy.

A divisive figure, Donald Trump surprised the Western powers, who were disappointed by his intention to promote his country's interests to the full, even if it meant threatening to destabilize traditional alliances and international organizations such as NATO, for which he considered his country's funding effort to be exaggeratedly high in comparison with the contributions of other member states. He also supported the Brexit. [36] Finally, he wanted to build a more flexible dialogue with Russia, while he was suspected of having received benevolent help from Moscow to win the 2016 presidential election. The investigation led by Special Counsel Robert Mueller, a former FBI director, delivered in its conclusions an absence of sufficiently evidentiary elements to affirm that the New York businessman had indeed benefited, knowingly, from Russian assistance. However, the doubt remained. As a reminder, Russia had been in the news during the election campaign because of attempts to interfere characterized by hacking and other maneuvers related to the dissemination of information to impact the chances of victory of the

---

[36] Author's note: Brexit refers to the United Kingdom's withdrawal from the European Union.

Democratic candidate Hillary Clinton. However, despite the ongoing investigation by Robert Mueller, Donald Trump understood that he had the unconditional support of a part of the American population, which was important enough to make him a popular political figure because of his economic results in line with his campaign promises.

The price of oil was one of Donald Trump's campaign themes in the 2018 midterm elections. One of his leitmotifs was the desire for every American citizen to have access to the lowest cost at the pump. This meant that international trading prices had to be as low as possible. As the election approached, the global oil market had seen its trading prices rise to levels more acceptable to most producers but still fragile to ensure a balanced budget. In October 2018, that is the month before the election, WTI was trading between $70 and $75 per barrel. In early November 2018, it was trading at or below $60. Despite his efforts to impact the market and his election promise kept, the results did not ensure him a majority in both houses of Congress. The second half of his term was thus more difficult, as Democratic representatives were determined to find the element that would trigger impeachment proceedings... but the unthinkable happened with the irruption of Covid-19.

During his first three years in office, Donald Trump got his way as long as oil markets remained favorable to U.S. producers. With oil prices only occasionally but briefly rising above $75 per WTI barrel, international trading prices continued to trend downwards and therefore favored U.S. manufacturers over their competitors' interests. Covid-19 disrupted American plans. The pandemic spread on a large scale within a few weeks, with China being the original focus.

At the beginning of 2020, no one imagined that this health concern would take on such proportions in terms of public health, coercive decisions concerning deprivation of freedom of individuals' movement and disastrous consequences on the world economy. The first weeks of the pandemic's "discovery" in the West led to unprecedented situations with the imposition of periods of confinement of the population and the sudden drop in economic activity in most of the countries affected by this plague. The oil sector did not escape the trend of the moment. China dealt the first blow to this market by drastically reducing its demand for black gold while it was the world's largest importer. By brutally cutting its demand by several million barrels per day, this decision quickly influenced trading prices, which immediately tended to fall. No one knew then that the effects of the pandemic would be felt for so long. Western Europe had no choice but to face a severe economic downturn, which was also characterized by a sharp drop in demand for black gold. For the oil sector, the situation became untenable as supply did not fall in proportion to demand. In mid-February 2020, Brent and WTI barrels were still trading above $55. In early March, they were around $40 and fell below $30 in early April.

Meanwhile, Covid-19 was ravaging everything in its path, while the human toll was increasing dramatically every new day around the world. For the oil industry, the situation looked like an industrial disaster because of the fall in prices, but also because of another, lesser-known factor: the risk of saturation of storage capacities around the world. This was another consequence of the imbalance in supply compared to demand. In mid-April 2020, the unthinkable happened when WTI reached a negative trading price... Never seen before. By then, panic had spread to many U.S. producers who were then producing at a dangerous loss. Many companies resigned themselves to slowing down their activity if they were not forced to stop it permanently. The first quarter of 2020 saw the U.S. oil industry falter and then collapse as well as well closures and mass layoffs. Policymakers were stunned to see the extent of the damage. Donald Trump was looking ahead to the 2020 presidential election in November and could not lose the support of the oil lobby.

Meanwhile, in March, the Saudis and the Russians failed to agree on a policy of lowering production to allow a rebound in exchange prices. On the contrary, Saudi Arabia showed its dissatisfaction by embarking on an aggressive price policy that precipitated their irretrievable fall in addition to the global decline in demand ... When I mention a watering can scenario, I am referring to the situation in which Donald Trump had no choice but to sound the alarm and urge his competitors to dialogue to find a way out of the crisis as soon as possible, forced to take the first step. He who had ardently campaigned for an oil policy that favored low exchange prices was forced to put an end to a situation that precipitated the bankruptcy of many American companies. The major international oil companies drastically reduced production. Trading prices gradually recovered and fluctuated between $35 and $40 per barrel until the presidential election of November 2020, which saw the victory of Joe Biden, the Democratic candidate opposed to Donald Trump. The outgoing President was criticized for his management of the Covid-19 crisis.

The arrival of Joe Biden as Head of the U.S. executive branch was like déjà vu four years earlier with the election of Donald Trump. In January 2021, he took on his new role and made a significant diplomatic shift towards his European allies. Relations with Russia became more strained, while it was important for him to signal to China that he did not intend to become the U.S. President who would symbolize the loss of political and economic leadership. As for energy and the fight against climate change, he immediately followed in the footsteps of Barack Obama. In fact, during his election campaign, he denounced climate change and said he wanted to tackle fossil fuels.

As it stands, President Biden has embarked on an oil policy like those deployed by Barack Obama and Donald Trump of maintaining a high production course. The motivations, once again, have not been dictated by a blatant and intentional lie; they stem from an economic and geopolitical reality that requires the United States to resort to this scenario to serve its strategic interests. It seems to me that Joe Biden really wants to fight climate change, but that the global geopolitical configuration dictates that he revises his initial plans concerning the production of oil made in the United States. Let's remember that he won the presidential election of November 2020 in a noxious atmosphere as his opponent had announced in advance that he would contest the election results in the event of a defeat... which he did not fail to do by triggering numerous legal proceedings, none of which ended up in his favor. Everyone remembers the amazing images of January 6, 2021, and the storming of the Capitol by Donald Trump's supporters who refused to recognize Joe Biden's victory. All of this occurred two weeks before the official inauguration of the new President-elect, while his predecessor was absent from the ceremony that traditionally symbolizes the passing of the baton of continuity in democratic governance. The former Vice-President under Barack Obama took over the reins of a country plagued by great internal problems, a nation deeply divided by racial issues, by a large-scale economic uncertainty resulting from the Covid-19 health crisis, and so on. As for the international scene, many doubted Joe Biden's ability to establish himself as a major international political leader. Some said he was getting old, while others worried about his mental health... I depart from these considerations and focus on a more pragmatic analysis of the situation: the forty-sixth President-elect in U.S. history was eagerly awaited both at home and on the international stage. He had to quickly assert his personality and his style, display his determination and ambitions. In this logic, he made a rapprochement with the traditional partners of the United States and immediately expressed his doubts or fears concerning Russia and China.

On February 23, 2022, the US Energy Information Administration [37] published a report on U.S. oil production projections. [38] Firstly, the date of publication deserves special attention because a few hours later, on the night of 23-24 February, Russia launched its military intervention in Ukraine. For several weeks, U.S. intelligence agencies had been convinced of an imminent military operation in Eastern Europe. However, the federal statistical agency was predicting a long-term increase in crude oil production to 2050, above the levels corresponding to Joe Biden's official assumption of office in the White House. In other words, this long-term trend did not emanate from a reflection based on current events, but from an analysis of the economic situation, which implied considering major trends.

Secondly, the war in Ukraine has reshuffled many cards. For a year now, a murderous war has been raging in this country, causing great concern in the Western world, which has strongly condemned the intervention carried out by the Kremlin. This war has had consequences for energy since the United States and its European allies quickly sought to weaken the Russian economy by attacking its hydrocarbon exports and imposing sanctions that went as

---

[37] Author's note: This is a federal agency dedicated to statistics within the Department of Energy. It was created by the U.S. Congress in 1977.
[38] *Petroleum and other liquids*, www.eia.gov, February 2022, p. 6

far as banning the import of these products from Russia. With the benefit of a few months' hindsight, the sanctions may not have had the desired effect in the short term, as Russia is still able to circumvent the sanctions by turning to other buyers. On the other hand, a major problem began to emerge in Europe as autumn approached: what about oil and gas supplies in the event of a harsh winter? Indeed, the Old Continent depends on hydrocarbon imports, a significant part of which comes from Russia. It was therefore necessary to find a way to compensate for the cessation of Russian supplies. Who could take advantage of the situation? The United States was not asking for much to gain market share in Europe.

The reality of the global oil market must be observed pragmatically. The war in Ukraine and the sanctions imposed by the Western world against Russia have further complicated a market already under pressure. For European states concerned about securing their supplies, the debate on diversifying strategic partnerships is back on the agenda. This requires developing these partnerships with other suppliers to reduce dependence on Russian oil as much as possible. This is a little more complicated to implement because when one reports the production of black gold, one does not indicate whether the producer has reached its maximum production capacity. On the other hand, it is also necessary to consider the route that the raw material must take to reach its destination. Finally, when one looks at the list of the ten countries with the largest proven oil reserves in the world, one realizes that five of them cannot fully exploit their natural resources for various reasons: economic insecurity, war or political and economic sanctions prevent Venezuela, Iraq, Iran, Russia and Libya from supplying the world market with what they would hope to produce in order to generate welcome revenues for their national economic health.

In this global context favorable to the United States, the latter has the luxury of being able to increase its production because it has not reached its maximum capacity in this area. Thus, the current state of the market fully benefits American producers, who rely on the green light from the executive branch to produce accordingly and influence the global game. They benefit at all levels. In Washington, they are happy to disrupt Russian energy plans and to titillate Beijing by showing their power in such a strategic market for which China is not competing. As for the producers, they are increasing their volumes produced and sold in a trading price configuration that they gladly bless. For the White House, this is obviously an ideal scenario since the country is placing its strategic pawns on the international chessboard while manufacturers are taking advantage of the situation to conquer market share and generate extraordinary revenues. Everyone benefits. So why stop?

The fight against global warming has not been called into question since it is still part of the Biden Administration's concerns. The United States is pursuing its policy of massive investments in energy programs that are part of an energy transition logic. On the other hand, for obvious economic, geopolitical, and geostrategic reasons, it does not want to miss the opportunity to benefit from its oil production, which allows it to maintain a strong influence but also a constant pressure in the power games that drive international relations. In this sense, the fight against climate change comes up against a major obstacle: political and economic pragmatism. While an energy policy is openly promoted in one direction, other energy policies that are the opposite of the issues officially opposed are simultaneously supported or promoted because of divergent interests that play the role of the priority of the moment. But

with oil, this famous priority of the moment is generally
sustainable.

84

The chiefs' fight for Arctic resources

This is a vast region, inhospitable because of its harsh climate, but whose rich soil and seabed attract the covetousness of many international actors. The Arctic does not only concern its coastal states. Although it is difficult to assess with certainty the state of its natural wealth, one does know that this Northern geographical area abounds in hydrocarbons and minerals. This region is also of concern to the scientific community because of the long-term trends in global warming. If human reason tends to be concerned about the environmental future of the planet, it is thwarted by other interests or issues that do not plead for its defense.

When one thinks about the Arctic, different images come to mind. The cold, the permafrost, the fauna specific to this type of environment or the low population density justifying the desert landscapes as far as the eye can see symbolize as much the gigantism and the beauty of the place as its inhospitality. The agglomerations exceeding one hundred thousand inhabitants are rare. The Russian cities of Murmansk and Norilsk remain exceptions. As for their little sisters Vorkuta and Apatity, they have a local population of about sixty thousand inhabitants, like the Norwegian city of Tromsø. In many parts of the Arctic, the population density is much lower than one person per square kilometer.

To exploit its natural resources, Russia offers its citizens to live in remote areas with attractive salaries promised to those tempted by the adventure of the great cold. Cities are developing there. However, when one consults the geopolitical news, one immediately understands that Russian supplies of hydrocarbons to Western and Central Europe mainly come from the Arctic region. In other words, the sanctions applied by the United States and its European partners are upsetting Russia's economic order... This amounts to forgetting that Russia has been looking to the East for nearly a decade.

Experts in the geopolitics of energy will not fail to point out that most of the Russian pipeline networks were initially intended to supply Europe with hydrocarbons, whereas the Eastern part of Russia is largely devoid of this type of infrastructure to transport them to China in particular. This consideration takes us away from the original idea of this chapter: the Arctic... Really? On closer inspection, not as much as one might imagine. Pipeline networks are certainly a major issue when it comes to supplies. However, global warming brings together many issues. Rising temperatures are impacting areas that are continuously frozen. Permafrost is melting in some Russian regions. The same is true for the ice in the northernmost seas of the world, which at this rate will allow the opening of new waterways. Thus, imagine the time savings that these future Arctic maritime highways will give to shipowners compared to traditional routes through warm seas. Think of the opportunities for Russia and China for oil and gas supplies. When analyzing an oil or gas pipeline project, one must consider the regions crossed, the topography of the terrain, the risks of political or social instability, the length of the pipe or even the climatic conditions that considerably increase the costs of construction, operation, and maintenance of the infrastructure. The maritime option therefore makes sense despite the many obstacles that still push shipowners to use traditional maritime routes.

Above all, it remains important to understand that the Arctic is like a great tectonic game with an obvious geostrategic dimension. Climate change, the war in Ukraine, the sensitive relations between several riparian countries and the prospect of exploiting abundant natural resources are all whetting appetites. Russia is undoubtedly the most active Arctic power in this area, the one that is provoking others to the point of shocking them and causing concern in the international community. Moreover, many wonder about the real motives of the Kremlin, which is facing the risk of natural disasters due to global warming while promoting the continuation of activities that are supposedly harmful to the environment. There is a real Moscow concern about the thawing of permafrost and the danger of landslides near inhabited areas, considering moreover that these natural phenomena can reach nuclear facilities. This consideration is counterbalanced by other decisions that deviate from environmental concerns. It is necessary to exploit the natural resources that contribute greatly to the proper functioning of the national economy. It is also important to occupy humanely almost deserted areas... and to militarize them.

This last point highlights the real desires of the Kremlin: by opting for such a policy, Russia is banking on hard power. Its official communication makes no doubt on the subject. The human forces present on the ground as well as the equipment and armaments are readily displayed to show to anyone its ambitions turned towards expansionism. The Arctic is a choice piece for Moscow, which is nothing new for Vladimir Putin.

In August 2007, the world was stunned by the news that a scientific expedition had just planted a flag of the Russian Federation at the exact location of the North Pole, at a depth of over four thousand meters. The Mir-1 bathyscaphe achieved this technical feat. Moreover, the name of this small submersible seems intended to send a message. Indeed, the word *mir* has two possible translations: peace and world. About the media coverage of the event, the symbolism of this expedition aimed at spreading a message oriented towards the spirit of conquest. Since then, Russia has not ceased to communicate in the sense of asserted territorial ambitions in this geographical area supposed to contain immense natural resources. The obvious interest is economic, but in view of the quality of the other riparian countries, it obviously covers a geopolitical dimension. To put it another way, in the eyes of the Kremlin, the Arctic is the best way to make the Western world sweat. It is therefore not surprising that Russia provokes its detractors by playing with the international rules of the law of the sea and claims of sovereignty. It relies particularly on the loopholes of the Montego Bay Convention, signed in November 1982, drafted under the United Nations Convention on the Law of the Sea (UNCLOS). It codifies the law of the sea, as well as the rights and duties of each country within the maritime space divided into several zones. Criteria for the delimitation of the zones have been agreed upon but are sometimes contested based on geological arguments. It is through this argument that Russia claims a more extensive sovereignty in the Arctic maritime space. Thus, it advocates an interpretation of this convention in the sense of an extended maritime sovereignty, while its detractors oppose it regarding the public international law in force. In other words, the whole debate is based on the problem of interpretation. This strategy is intended to irritate the other riparian countries, starting with the United States, which is not a signatory to the Montego Bay Convention. The latter are bound by other consensual texts related to the law of the sea, but not the UNCLOS. In short, Moscow's attitude is strangely reminiscent of the Cold War, especially since, despite the Ukrainian conflict which mobilizes the bulk of the Russian army, the Kremlin deploys armed forces in unoccupied regions and communicates on the quality of the weaponry accompanying them. In this sense, the Russian ambitions worry the concert of nations, which wonders about the country's true intentions.

The scenario of a militarized conflict in the Arctic seems unlikely given the war in Ukraine, the forces mobilized, and the economic efforts made. However, because of the uncertainty surrounding the Kremlin's true intentions, several littoral states have opted for an attitude of preparation for the most bellicose scenarios. NATO is conducting training missions near the Russian border to counter any form of adverse military action. The ambient climate has gradually taken a much more anxious turn. The fears are such that they do not only concern the other countries bordering the Arctic and members of the Arctic Council. [39] As you can see, Russian communication operations are making the Atlantic Alliance very sensitive... which is undoubtedly the expected goal. This attitude defended by Vladimir Putin is part of his global vision which includes an expansionist will in line with his dream of restoring the grandeur of the tsarist empire and this absolute determination to show that Russia belongs to the cenacle of the dominant powers of the planet.

This last statement highlights a fixed idea that obsesses the mind of Vladimir Putin expressed since the 2000s. Nothing and no one will dictate to Russia what to do. This positioning has allowed him to play on the patriotic fiber and to attract the favor of the Russian people. Despite the war in Ukraine, he remains popular because his fellow citizens see in him the incarnation of the desired leader, that of an ardent defender of the image of Russia and its

---

[39] Author's note: Briefly, since 1996 and the Ottawa Declaration on its establishment, the Arctic Council includes Russia, Canada, the United States, Norway, Sweden, Finland, Iceland, and Denmark. This multi-stakeholder council promotes sustainable development in the Arctic in the social, economic, and environmental fields.

grandeur. Thus, his ambitions on the Arctic are hardly surprising when one considers his vision of the multipolarity of the world. By multipolarity, one must understand that Vladimir Putin identifies several poles dominating the world and that he includes his country in the circle of major powers of the planet. This speech has several messages. Firstly, the one that affirms Russia's place in the international arena. Secondly, it addresses the Western world and more particularly NATO [40] , meaning that Moscow has arguments to put forward if necessary. In other words, it refers to the military dimension. Thirdly, beyond any form of warning, the Russian leader speaks like a conqueror. He is not content with warnings but goes on the offensive.

In the Arctic, the mission in charge of planting the Russian flag at the North Pole did not have as its only objective to expose the technical prowess of the Russian scientific community. It had to mark the spirits by displaying its ambitions and its conquering desires. For the past fifteen years, tensions have been growing in the region because of Moscow's maritime claims. The establishment of a human and above all military presence in desert areas has constituted a new threshold obviously perceived with concern by the other riparian countries and NATO. Considering the recurrent tensions between Russia and Ukraine since Vladimir Putin's first presidential term and, above all, the escalation of threats up to the outbreak of an

---

[40] Author's note: Not all countries bordering the Arctic region are members of NATO. Due to the war in Ukraine and threats from Moscow, Sweden and Finland have expressed their willingness to join the Atlantic Alliance. On the other hand, the two countries mentioned are part of the EU. To put it differently, in the event of a Russian act of war against one of these two countries, there is no doubt that Russia would be exposed to a coalition response.

armed conflict, are there any limits to the Kremlin's provocations regarding the Arctic?

The high human and logistical mobilization and the cost of the war effort in Ukraine may lead one to believe that a new war in the northernmost regions of the planet would be a risky option for its decision-maker, given the pedigree of the riparian states and the alliance games that unite them. In this sense, the probability seems to me to be low, if not totally excluded. On the other hand, it is important for Moscow to show its strength on such inhospitable terrain. In this case, the official communication displays an image of elite troops, of modern and state-of-the-art weaponry, which contrasts with the image conveyed by the difficulties encountered by the Russian army in Ukraine and the comments about the poverty or even the obsolescence of the equipment, the unpreparedness, and the inexperience of the combatant formations. As soon as Russia deploys armed forces in its most remote Arctic regions, the other riparian countries understand that regional geopolitics takes on a much more critical dimension since it now involves hard power. In other words, the Kremlin does not intend to limit itself to maritime claims with the sole aim of recovering the exclusive exploitation of subsoils full of natural resources. While economic perspectives certainly count for a lot in Moscow's provocations, the geopolitical dimension cannot be overlooked. The latter is part of the challenge to the paradigm of Western world domination in international relations. This line of thought has naturally declined with the rise in political and economic power of China. However, Vladimir Putin does not imply any Chinese-Russian alliance when he speaks of multipolarity. In his eyes, Russia constitutes a pole. This vision certainly influences Russian provocations in the Arctic... which do not displease China, a country that intends to continue its commercial exchanges with Russia in view of securing its oil supplies.

Very briefly, it is estimated that the Arctic is home to nearly 13% of the world's black gold reserves [41] , voluminous natural gas reserves are yet to be discovered and rare minerals are the focus of increasingly fierce international competition. While the scientific world is crying out to denounce the consequences of global warming and the risks likely to threaten the life or survival of many ecosystems, the prevailing geopolitical context hardly encourages caution regarding the over-exploitation of natural resources. While state leaders are officially promoting public policies aimed at reducing our dependence on hydrocarbons, other economic and political realities favor the rush to lucrative and safe havens. Once again, I refuse to use the word *hypocrisy*; our operating model is based on the identification of problems that one tries to slow down, reduce, or even annihilate, while others require means of action or intervention that cancel out the efforts made for the former. This is called realpolitik. The Arctic illustrates this apparently schizophrenic thinking in some respects, but it is certainly realistic in view of the stakes placed in the balance. One denounces the rise in temperatures in the region. One is concerned about the accelerated melting of the ice caps. One wonders about the future living conditions of polar bears. And so on. All this is true. However, the antagonistic interests of some and others make that one talks a lot about these problems whereas others acquire sufficient importance so that solutions at the antipodes of the prerequisites and common sense are promoted in fine. To be clear, I expose two ideas thought in their time by eminent philosophers. On the one hand, I refer to Thomas Hobbes and his *Leviathan* [42] in which he

---

[41] *"Épisode 3/3 : Arctique : les gisements de toutes les convoitises,"* www.radiofrance.fr, February 15, 2023

postulates that man is a wolf for man. On the other hand, fans of Nietzsche will recognize the "human, too human" dimension. In other words, the future of indigenous populations, local fauna and flora seem to weigh the equivalent of miserable cotton sacks compared to the real political, geopolitical, and economic interests disputed by public and private actors from the four corners of the planet. The war in Ukraine and the problems linked to European hydrocarbon supplies have pushed Norway to look for new deposits to exploit to compensate for the shortfall in Russian gas deliveries. However, this Scandinavian kingdom is known for its public policies defending the environment. The current circumstances have changed Oslo's habits, and it no longer views the opportunity to take market share from the Old Continent with a negative eye.

I will voluntarily move away from oil issues and focus my attention on a territory that attracts many eyes because of its abundant natural resources. Greenland is somewhat of an exception in a world where the defense of economic and strategic interests is paramount. This autonomous territory, which still belongs to the Danish crown, has refused any form of activity related to oil or gas. As far as black gold is concerned, estimates indicate that there are several tens of billions of barrels of exploitable reserves. Such a statistic is a challenge. Greenland lives essentially thanks to the annual subsidies allocated by Copenhagen. However, such supposed reserves represent a real economic treasure in the making. The local political elites have decided otherwise. In July 2021, they opted to ban all onshore and offshore oil exploration. Two major reasons influenced this choice: the risks of environmental damage and the low profitability of oil activity. At such Northern latitudes, the investments required for oil

---

[42] Thomas Hobbes, *Leviathan or The Matter, Forme and Power of a Commonwealth Ecclesiasticall and Civil*, London, 1651

exploration and the production costs offer reduced profitability prospects for this economic sector. As for the ecological dimension, the local ruling elites have acted with conviction. They are genuinely concerned about the environmental consequences of developing this type of activity. A few months later, in November, the Greenlandic Parliament promoted a law prohibiting the exploration and exploitation of uranium on its territory, while estimates indicate that the reserves are equivalent to several hundred thousand tons that can be exploited, considering that world and annual production in recent years has fluctuated between fifty-five thousand and sixty-five thousand tons. [43] Thus, local public decision-makers are promoting legislation in the direction of environmental protection...

My critical mind approves Greenland's initiatives in this area but wonders about the political and legal future of this territory, which will eventually become independent. In such a case, the country will have to become economically self-sufficient, as independence would probably include an end to Danish subsidies. The current parliamentary majority, which ardently defends the independence aspiration, refuses to exploit potentially lucrative natural resources for its local economy. What will be the economic model? Tourism is beginning to develop, but it remains insufficient to support the economic needs of the Greenlandic nation. Similarly, the national authorities, based in Nuuk, were disappointed with the occurrence of the Covid-19 crisis when China imposed restrictions on fisheries imports that accounted for 90% of the island's exports [44] and caused significant drops in revenue. It is

---

[43] *"La production d'uranium,"* www.iaea.org, accessed on March 14, 2023

[44] Mathieu Landriault, Jean-François Savard, Anna Soer, Julie Renaud, *"L'indépendance du Groenland : un mouvement qui a le vent dans les voiles,"* cqegheiulaval.com, RG v8n1, 2022

therefore important to find ways to diversify its local economy and to turn to new international markets. In this sense, Greenland expects to continue its good trade relations with China and has opened an embassy there in 2021. [45] It also hopes to build and expand trade partnerships with South Korea and Japan.

Very briefly, the population of the island does not exceed fifty-seven thousand souls for a territory exceeding two million square kilometers. The density of population is thus very weak. As for the exploitation of natural resources, it seems currently condemned to remain in the state of buried projects because of the local political will to privilege the environmental interests. However, the Parliament has not completely closed the door to the future exploitation of certain minerals. Let's keep in mind that public policies and laws are not set in stone. Everything can change depending on the political leaders of the moment. In other words, there is no guarantee that Greenland will maintain this position indefinitely, even though its population is openly willing to defend the environment. This idea may have convinced the EU to continue its funding policy in Greenland, as well as the United States, which proposed a free trade agreement to Nuuk in 2021. In short, Europeans and Americans are working hard to prevent China from taking up strategic positions in the territory, particularly in terms of mining resources. Moreover, other foreign powers also covet these resources as soon as they have the attribute of scarcity. The Western world is clearly not interested in seeing Beijing advance its pawns in this region of the world. At the risk of being wrong, I have a hunch that Greenland will not become independent any time soon for these same strategic reasons. I quickly mentioned the low local population density. Let's

---

[45] *Ibid.*

imagine the economic necessity of exploiting mineral or hydrocarbon resources, major projects would require a large workforce. Westerners would certainly not approve the massive arrival of Chinese, Indian or other workers, but this would allow their country of origin to gain influence in Greenland.

The examples of the Russian expansionist will in the Arctic, or the Greenlandic case provide an overview of the multitude of political, economic, geopolitical, or geostrategic interests gravitating around this geographical area. There is no shortage of subjects of discord and tension. They do not only involve the countries bordering the Arctic. Other international actors are not insensitive to the interests they can gain by establishing commercial relations with some or by lurking in the shadows of the quarrels between the Arctic countries. Oil is rather discreet within this multitude of antagonistic interests. However, one should not remove it from the list of sensitive issues. It is part of the strategic issues that cause tensions. It is not the only coveted natural resource, but it is present in quantity, while the development of maritime trade in the northernmost seas of the planet makes it a key player in the strategic interests defended by the main political and economic powers. Meanwhile, the defenders of environmental causes are constantly sounding the alarm about the ecological disaster represented by the exploitation of black gold and, more generally, of all potentially exploitable natural resources.

Since the outbreak of war in Ukraine in February 2022, energy has been at the heart of the Old Continent's main concerns. How can it secure the oil and gas supplies formerly provided by Russia? When it comes to oil, one should not only consider the security dimension, which is far too simplistic. There are also economic opportunities for states and companies specializing in this sector of activity. Who would be deprived of them?

January 2023, the Norwegian government announced its intention to open a record number of blocks in the Arctic, all dedicated to hydrocarbon exploration. The official communication mentions ninety-two blocks, seventy-eight of which are in the Barents Sea. A record. However, if one refers to Norway, one is considering a country turned towards renewable energy. In fact, the country's largest employer is none other than Equinor, the giant company specializing in the wind energy sector... but not only. Equinor was formerly called Statoil before becoming StatoilHydro. To show the will of the country to turn to the so-called clean energies, one operated a change of name to confer a connotation more in adequacy with the environment and the ecology. By renaming the company Equinor, any sound or reference to the oil sector was removed. However, the Norwegian government has officially communicated in the sense of a prospecting dedicated to the search for hydrocarbons, a decision strongly criticized by environmental activists. Perhaps will it defend itself by invoking a circumstantial decision in view of the war in Ukraine? With such an argument, it would show above all that oil remains the unavoidable asset or the haven to be asserted, the one that far surpasses the choices of reason imploring a decarbonization of the world economy to meet the climate objectives defined at the last UN climate conferences. With oil, the god of money continues to flow freely. Business is business.

Black gold in the Washington-Beijing rivalry

The two main state superpowers of the planet are opposed to each other in many areas. China is no longer hiding its ambitions. To achieve this, it promotes outward-looking public policies. Its economic future will depend on its ability to export but also to import certain goods and services necessary to satisfy its economic growth plans. Oil has a special place here. It is a priority objective for Beijing since the needs satisfied by black gold are considerable and the country does not have the necessary resources within itself to satisfy them. It therefore buys from several suppliers, but this imperative involves a double problem. Firstly, it needs to buy large volumes. In 2022, it was importing almost eleven million barrels a day [46] , which represented three quarters of its needs. Secondly, given this dependence on external suppliers, it is important to secure its supplies. The pharaonic plan to restore the Silk Roads aims to facilitate China's trade with Asia, Europe, and Africa. It also seeks to build the communication routes that will ensure the necessary supplies of raw materials. They are already reconfiguring the global geopolitics of oil. To optimize the security of its black gold imports, Beijing is striving to reduce transport distances, hence the construction of numerous roads, railways, and port infrastructures to meet this objective. The national leaders hope to eliminate any risks by freeing themselves from routes that are considered difficult. The Strait of Malacca is a major issue, while it is notoriously insecure due to the piracy that plagues the region. However, a significant part of Chinese oil imports crosses this dreaded zone to reach its destination. Indeed, the Middle Kingdom buys part of its black gold from Middle Eastern producers. This fear

---

[46] Paul Louis, *"La Russie devient le premier fournisseur de pétrole de la Chine,"* www.bfmtv.com, June 20, 2022

explains why it is now turning to its Russian neighbor to buy oil, a strategic partner happy to trade with a state that has not sanctioned it regarding the war in Ukraine. However, all this is not enough to reassure President Xi Jinping. He relies on foreign trade for the smooth functioning of the national economy as well as on diplomacy. This novelty is not only intended to position China as a major global political power; it is also intended to destabilize American diplomacy, especially in the Middle East. Curiously, oil is at the heart of these intrigues worthy of *House of Cards*.

The famous Strait of Malacca is one of the most strategic crossing points in the world like Hormuz, Bab al-Mandab, Suez, and Panama canals. Most of the world's maritime transport transits through these places with a sometimes-tumultuous climate. They are among those geographical areas that are potentially harmful to international trade, especially oil trade, for various reasons. Piracy, diplomatic disputes, and other factors sometimes lead to local disruptions that can quickly lead to larger-scale consequences. The Strait of Malacca runs along the coasts of four countries: Indonesia, Singapore, Thailand, and Malaysia. It stretches for five hundred and eighty-five miles. It has long had a reputation as a region of insecurity and piracy, to the extent that it has been considered for the creation of other passageways such as the Kra Canal in Thailand. The number of acts of piracy has decreased in recent years, as indicated by the French Ministry of the Armed Forces. *"If the Strait of Malacca has long been subject to very active piracy, the latest report of the MICA Center (Maritime Information Cooperation and Awareness Center) now considers that it is no longer a "risk zone". Criminal activities have in fact moved to the Singapore Strait, its extension."* [47] However, the security progress observed does not absolve the region of the evils that threaten its precarious geopolitical balance. Piracy therefore remains an existing danger, just as diplomatic tensions can ignite the area at any time. China knows this perfectly well since most of its oil imports pass through this strait. It has chosen to reduce its dependence on this strategic passage. On the other hand, it has not yet found the right solution because the other options being promoted do not offer any guarantee of security for the transportation of black gold to its oil terminals. It has opted for the civilian and military port terminal of Gwadar in Pakistan, but the rail and road links to China run through Baluchistan, a region known for its instability. China has also developed an Economic Corridor with Myanmar [48], which provides an outlet to the Bay of Bengal and the Indian Ocean. However, Beijing is also thinking about other projects. The nation's capital is looking to deploy different supply routes throughout Asia to guard against any disruptive contingencies such as India. Asia's other demographic giant does not have good diplomatic relations with its Chinese neighbor. Both countries are massing troops in the Himalayan border areas. Armed clashes sometimes punctuate peaks of tension that give rise to the dreaded assumption that the situation is out of control. Moreover, the Chinese-Pakistani roads strongly displease New Delhi, which considers that they cross regions claimed by the Indian power center... The regional climate does not lend itself to appeasement. Numerous

---

[47] *"Avril 2022: le détroit de Malacca,"* www.defense.gouv.fr, accessed April 5, 2023. Original version : « *Si le détroit de Malacca a longtemps été soumis à une piraterie très active, le dernier rapport du MICA Center (Maritime Information Cooperation and Awareness Center) considère aujourd'hui qu'il n'est plus une « zone à risque. » »*. Les activités criminelles se seraient en effet déplacées vers le détroit de Singapour, son prolongement. »

[48] Author's note: The China-Myanmar Economic Corridor refers to various infrastructure projects which support connectivity between the two countries among the Belt and Road Initiative.

rivalries mark the geopolitics of the Persian Gulf, the Indian subcontinent, and Southeast Asia. All of this has led China to develop infrastructure projects in Central Asia and to turn to Russia, which sees Beijing as an opportunity to get around Western sanctions on hydrocarbon exports. However, the authorities intend to diversify supply options and reduce the weight of the Strait of Malacca through which nearly 80% of Chinese oil imports pass.

Between Washington and Beijing, there is no shortage of subjects of discord. Both seek to antagonize their rival and weaken it. In this tense context, the United States has a choice advantage in terms of its oil reserves and its weight on the international markets. The country has never exported so much black gold and is reaping considerable profits. The war in Ukraine and the sanctions in force against Russian hydrocarbon exports favor American interests which, opportunistically, are taking advantage of the situation to strengthen their commercial links with their European partners. On the other hand, although eager to harm Chinese interests by making it difficult for them to access oil, their diplomatic influence is reaching its limits regarding the strategic partnerships agreed by Beijing with Moscow, Tehran, or Riyadh. In this great game of chess, each side deploys its strategy to destabilize the other. Americans and Chinese are advancing their pawns. All moves are permitted. They berate each other over heated issues such as Taiwan, the Huawei affair, or customs tariffs. They intimidate each other. Dialogue seems difficult as during the bilateral meeting organized in Anchorage, Alaska, in March 2021. The representatives of the two countries broke away from the customary friendliness in such circumstances and displayed a coldness that characterized an obvious distance. The tone was set two months after Joe Biden took office in the White House. Among the grievances outlined by Washington, the fate of the Uighurs in Xinjiang, Hong Kong, the former Formosa, and the cyber-attacks against the United States were intended to lay the foundations for a meeting that the latter hoped constructive. This speech displeased the Chinese delegation, which retaliated by calling on its interlocutor to change its image in the world and to stop promoting its democracy outside its borders. Criticism came from both sides and showed above all that each camp intended to stick to its position. China did not intend to be intimidated in this way, sure of its strength. However, at the end of the meeting, both countries communicated in the sense of a useful meeting based on frank and constructive exchanges. Diplomatic common sense thus regained the upper hand, only apparently and temporarily. Cases of discord have not failed to spice up these tumultuous diplomatic relations since then.

The case of Taiwan has been a source of heated opposition between Beijing and Washington for several decades. The first mentioned country considers Taipei as an integral part of the People's Republic of China. It recognizes neither its independence nor its sovereignty. The latter, on the other hand, is concerned about China's intentions towards Taiwan. As things stand, one trend is becoming increasingly clear: many countries are breaking off diplomatic relations with the small island in the China Sea, anxious to maintain cordial ties with Beijing. The Taiwanese authorities, however, refuse to accept the idea of "reintegrating" into the Chinese fold. They consider themselves independent and are striving to continue their experiment in democratic governance of the regime. They have the support of the United States, which has made the island a model political regime. For several years, Beijing and Washington have been eyeing each other on the Taiwanese issue. Tensions have increased and become more intense as soon as they involve the military dimension. The provocations come from both sides. They resemble a game of ping-pong. In September 2022, a few weeks before the mid-term elections, the then Speaker of the House of Representatives, Democratic Nancy Pelosi, maintained her plan to travel to Taipei to openly show her support for the local authorities... a trip perceived by Beijing yet another American provocation. The Chinese capital responded by launching military maneuvers near the Taiwanese coast, thus sanctioning the temerity of the former number three in the U.S. organization chart. In addition to the electoral perspective, Nancy Pelosi's visit came at an extremely sensitive time. War had been raging in Eastern Europe for nearly seven months, but everyone remembered the joint statement made by Xi Jinping and Vladimir Putin on the sidelines of the opening ceremony of the Beijing Winter Olympics. Both sent a message to the Western world denouncing the existence of NATO as an anachronistic relic of the Cold War, while the Chinese leader attacked the AUKUS [49] , the tripartite military cooperation between the United States, the United Kingdom and Australia. At the time of the incident, U.S. intelligence agencies had already warned of an imminent risk of a Russian-orchestrated military attack in Ukraine. The message issued by the two heads of the Russian and Chinese governments confirmed the growing schism in the international community by commenting on *"the entry of international affairs into a new era."* [50] They issued a blunt warning to the Western powers that the paradigm of their dominance was coming to an end. Less than three weeks later, Vladimir Putin launched hostilities in Ukraine. He made good on his

---

[49] Author's note: AUKUS refers to a tripartite military cooperation agreement aimed at containing Chinese expansionism in the Indo-Pacific arc. It was made public in September 2021.

[50] Benoît Vitkine, Frédéric Lemaître, *"Aux JO de Pékin, Vladimir Poutine et Xi Jinping s'affichent en leaders d'un monde post-occidental,"* www.lemonde.fr, February 5, 2022

threats. As for China, the Taiwan crisis was causing much concern in the West. Everyone wondered about Xi Jinping's true intentions. Would he in turn challenge the United States and its allies to an armed conflict in the Far East? As a fine strategist, he maneuvered skillfully. China did not have the warmongering reputation of its Russian neighbor, but its defense budget continued to grow. In 2023, it will increase by 7.2% [51] compared to the previous year, which will raise many questions in the Western camp. To date, Chinese military maneuvers near the Taiwanese coast have not amused anyone in Washington. This annoyance also concerns Chinese activities in the South China Sea. At the end of April 2023, American authorities took exception to the activities of a coastguard vessel from the Asian giant that almost collided with a Philippine ship. [52] Beijing was not moved by the U.S. warnings. On the contrary, the two-time Olympic city is in the spirit of the famous Latin saying *si vis pacem, para bellum* [53] while showing off its latest weaponry.

The technological rivalry between the world's two largest economies is becoming more intense. Innovation is one of the ingredients that boost a country's hard and soft powers. China is now communicating on its technological progress, particularly in the military field. It is openly displaying its ambitions in the field of space conquest. This sector requires a level of expertise and financing capacities that only the most powerful countries manage to promote and mobilize. Similarly, the Huawei affair still haunts the minds of Westerners. If the background of the case is based

---

[51] *"La Chine augmente son budget militaire pour 2023,"* www.france24.com, March 5, 2023

[52] Le Figaro and AFP, *"Washington appelle Pékin à cesser son action « dangereuse » en mer de Chine méridionale,"* www.lefigaro.fr, April 29, 2023

[53] Author's note: "If you want peace, prepare for war".

on a dark accusation of espionage by the United States and several of its traditional allies, I felt more like a wind of panic swept through the West when Beijing announced that it could deploy its 5G technology throughout the world. Maybe I am wrong, but I am still wondering if the Western world had taken the measure of the real Chinese technological progress. I am only speculating, and I do not know for sure, but the mastery of 5G has raised the most serious fears outside China. The facts reveal an irrefutable truth: Chinese high technology rivals that of the most advanced powers in this field. However, I keep in mind that scientific and technological progress does not annihilate the shortcomings of mastery and control of the latter. My gaze falls on the mysterious case of the Covid-19 health crisis. For many months, the world speculated about the true origins of this pandemic disease that spread around the world. Today, according to the FBI, the most likely explanation is a laboratory accident [54] but should be treated with caution. [55] This human tragedy has caused the death of several million people worldwide. In the United States, under the Trump presidency, China was even suspected of having deliberately manufactured a virus intended to kill, a suspicion that further fueled the intense tensions in relations between the two countries. This health case still has some grey areas. In addition to the human toll, it has caused considerable economic damage, with many jurisdictions facing recession. Donald Trump's mishandling of the pandemic is likely to have influenced the American vote for Joe Biden in 2022. As for Xi Jinping, although he confirmed that he would retain his leadership in October 2022 at the conclusion of the Chinese Communist Party's

---

[54] Le Temps and AFP, *"Origines du Covid-19 : aux États-Unis, la thèse du laboratoire refait surface au ministère de l'Énergie,"* www.letemps.ch, February 26, 2023

[55] William Audureau, *"Origines du Covid-19 : pourquoi il faut rester prudent,"* www.lemonde.fr, March 2, 2023

twentieth National Congress, he has also been the subject of criticism among his own people.

There is one area where the two rivals do not operate on an equal footing: oil. Both have oil and are among the world's largest producers. As I have shown in previous chapters, the United States relies on its shale oil exports to influence world markets. In the world of large holders of black gold, many are unable to produce or export at will. On the other hand, for the past three decades, China's oil needs have reached such proportions that domestic production is no longer sufficient to satisfy the domestic market. In this sense, the United States has an advantage that it is exploiting extensively, as its goal remains to thwart China's access to oil. I stress that the weight of oil in the balance of the Chinese-American rivalry should not be underestimated. If the Middle Kingdom were no longer able to import what it needs, the dynamism of its national model would quickly be impacted and characterized by slowed economic growth. It is therefore important to secure its import networks and the volumes that are essential to its economic functioning. This imperative partly motivates its diplomacy around the world. Although oil alone does not explain the choices made by Beijing internationally, it remains at the heart of its concerns and motivates commercial relations abhorred by Washington, such as the purchase of black gold from Iran. In short, oil justifies a Chinese diplomacy designed to annoy the American ruling elites. When the latter threaten anyone with reprisals for doing business with Tehran, Beijing does not care about these intimidations, which the Chinese capital does not consider. It advances where its interests take it. It does not intend to give in to any American warning, especially when oil appears in the background.

China has recently entered a field that it was not previously known for: that of diplomatic mediator. When Donald Trump succeeded in validating the Abraham Accords in August 2020, he achieved a real diplomatic feat by bringing together the State of Israel and several Arab powers in the region, led by Saudi Arabia. One argument was enough to convince them to re-establish dialogue: they were all fighting against a common enemy, Iran. In March 2023, the Western world was petrified by the news. China had just announced an unexpected diplomatic success in bringing Saudi Arabia and Iran together, all of which was done in Beijing. For Washington, this tour de force signed by Xi Jinping acted as an electroshock: Chinese diplomacy performed where the State Department had failed for several decades, regardless of the dominant political trend in the White House. Worse, Saudi Arabia had listened to Beijing. What conclusions should one draw from such a Chinese diplomatic success in the Middle East? It seems to me that it shows how difficult it is for the United States to make its voice heard in a region where Washington has made many mistakes over the past decades. The wars in Afghanistan and Iraq have contributed to the rise of anti-American sentiment in many Asian jurisdictions, especially in countries where Islamic culture predominates. Yet, by targeting Muslim Uighurs, China could expose itself to the rise of anti-Chinese sentiment. China does not seek to cultivate its popularity on the mainland. It relies on trade and does not care whether its partners like it or not. Many denounce its methods, but it continues to move forward, without blinking. On the American side, however, the White House and the State Department are certainly obsessed with a recurring question: how to slow down China's advances through its Silk Roads diplomacy? Similarly, the Saudi attitude raises many questions. Oil interests come into play since China buys oil from the Wahhabi kingdom. For its part, the Arab oil-monarchy has moderately appreciated the American policy of producing to favor the available supply and encourage the lowering of crude exchange prices. By doing so, the United States is harming Saudi economic interests. On the other hand, I suspect another motivation of Beijing-Riyadh rapprochement: Africa. Saudi Arabia expects to gain increasing diplomatic and economic weight on the entire continent. This ambition is motivated by the kingdom's desire to diversify its national economy and reduce its economic dependence on the oil sector. It is thus looking to other sectoral and geographical horizons. As for China, it would find in Saudi Arabia an ideal partner, one that would act as a privileged interlocutor for its African interests and allow it to advance its pawns more discreetly on a continent subject to numerous local and regional tensions and destabilizations. In a complex global geopolitical climate, I am not convinced that China would welcome the intervention of the decried Wagner troops in several African jurisdictions... although it does not intend to jeopardize its trade relations with Moscow, particularly regarding its hydrocarbon imports. On the other hand, I notice that the Western powers are losing influence in Africa. In this game of musical chairs, there will be winners and losers. In view of the new Silk Roads policies and China's positioning in the Middle East, I postulate that Beijing is aiming to increasingly secure its access to natural resources in Africa, an area where the United States' power of seduction seems limited.

Oil certainly holds a special place in the Chinese-American opposition, vital for both economic models as much as inescapable in their respective diplomacy. While I refuse to speculate on any kind of American decline in international relations, I note above all that China is continuing its rise to the top and is upsetting American interests in areas where it was not expected to be so enterprising and effective. Moreover, Beijing's diplomatic success with Riyadh and Tehran is not insignificant. In 2020, these two states, which were already selling oil to China, accounted for more than a quarter of the world's proven reserves of black gold. [56] Who could believe that oil interests were not part of Beijing's motivation in this diplomatic rapprochement? By alleviating one or more crisis areas in the Middle East, China may have laid the groundwork for an effective strategy to extinguish fires that could jeopardize its supplies, which are so essential to its economic functioning. In this case, although it has many oil partners, a significant part of its purchases come from these two countries. On this issue, the United States has obviously taken the brunt of the blow, but this is just one battle among many in a bilateral rivalry that is becoming more and more acute every day.

[56] Béatrice Mariais, *"Moyen-Orient et réserves de pétrole : les réserves des 20 premiers pays en 2020,"* www.lesclesdumoyenorient.com, November 11, 2021

Climate change versus political and economic pragmatism

In the worlds of political advice and parallel diplomacy, common sense does not always prevail in decisions. For every official explanation there is a much more unofficial reason, which is certainly decisive in the balance of pros and cons. The issue of climate change is no exception to this rule. Moreover, it continues to be the subject of controversy since its recognition is not unanimous. For some, this thesis has no place. It would be a lie, a fabrication or a manipulation intended to promote the emergence of a new economic model, to promote or defend the interests of certain public and private actors... Sometimes, one flirts with conspiracy theories to denounce the great deception relating to the alleged existence of climate change. One refuses to recognize any human responsibility. In other words, assuming that the warming of the Earth is considered, it could be due to a natural cause. In such a case, Man and his consumption habits are completely exonerated. More prosaically, the detractors of climate change rely mainly on one argument: doubt. This leads to a double difficulty: firstly, to prove the existence of global warming; secondly, to establish a link with a human activity. If no irrefutable scientific proof can be provided, the climate skeptics will fall back on the loophole of uncertainty. This strategy works. It annoys those who denounce the evils of climate change. It irritates those same people who regularly warn about the targets set at the annual COPs, relating to greenhouse gas emissions for example, and which have not been met. It despairs the experts who believe that there is danger in the house, that human activity holds a large share of responsibility among the causes of global warming. Among the designated culprits, oil figures prominently. It is blamed for its excessive consumption. It is hard to argue the contrary, since oil consumption has been increasing steadily for several decades and is still at levels that are inadequate in view of the recommendations to reduce greenhouse gas emissions. A vast undertaking. Big debate. Mad concerns about the future of life on Earth. An energy transition is necessary but not everyone is happy about it. Some people prefer to make the best of a bad situation... or so it seems. How many oil companies have opted to diversify their activities, notably towards clean energy, to meet the requirements defined at climate conferences and the texts agreed by their participants? Let's not lie to ourselves: these large companies will not soon give up their oil and gas business, which brings them so much profit and which still constitutes the bulk of their revenues. How many industries owe their economic success to the use of oil or its by-products?

At the United Nations General Assembly in September 2021, Secretary General Antonio Guterres gave an unequivocal opening address. *"I am here to sound the alarm: The world must wake up. We are on the edge of an abyss - and moving in the wrong direction. Our world has never been more threatened. Or more divided. We face the greatest cascade of crises in our lifetimes. [...] The climate crisis is pummeling the planet."* [57] [58] This message does not

---

[57] Antonio Guterres, opening speech of the general debate of the General Assembly, press.un.org, September 21, 2021

[58] *Ibidem*, the entire part of the speech related to the climate: *"The climate alarm bells are also ringing at fever pitch. The recent report of the Intergovernmental Panel on Climate Change was a code red for humanity. We see the warning signs in every continent and region. Scorching temperatures. Shocking biodiversity loss. Polluted air, water and natural spaces. And climate-related disasters at every turn. As we saw recently, not even this city — the financial capital of the world — is immune. Climate scientists tell us it's not too late to keep alive the 1.5 degree goal of the Paris Climate Agreement. But the window is rapidly closing. We need a 45 per cent cut in emissions by*

come from just anyone. It denounces the ever more worrying evils that threaten the future of life on Earth. The tone of the speech leaves no room for doubt: humanity is exposed to great peril if it does not change its consumption habits and behaviors. Antonio Guterres relies on serious scientific reports and cites the studies conducted by the IPCC. He urges the international community to promote the means to make a real energy transition and to recall the commitments made regarding agreed financing that have never been honored. In other words, he points to a collective responsibility and is concerned about the published results that fall far short of those defined to contain a phenomenon identified as harmful to humanity. Time is running out. If a reaction does not occur quickly, in the short term, climate change will tend to worsen with the consequences inherent in such a prospect. It is up to Man to equip himself with the necessary means to reverse a trend that seems uncertain. Once again, such a discourse confronts the common sense and the cold pragmatism of a multitude of political, economic, and other interests that do not agree with the exhortation to operate as soon as possible an energy transition to reduce greenhouse gas emissions. Our future belongs to us. It will depend on our choices. According to the scientific world, the situation remains reversible, but the room for maneuver is getting smaller and smaller.

When I mention antagonistic interests to the necessary actions to fight against climate change, I specify

---

2030. Yet a recent UN report made clear that with present national climate commitments, emissions will go up by 16% by 2030. That would condemn us to a hellscape of temperature rises of at least 2.7 degrees above pre-industrial levels. A catastrophe. Meanwhile, the OECD just reported a gap of at least $20 billion in essential and promised climate finance to developing countries. We are weeks away from the UN Climate Conference in Glasgow, but seemingly light years away from reaching our targets. We must get serious. And we must act fast."

that there are political and economic actors who are sincere in their willingness to commit to this great challenge. I do not wish to spread any message of generalization and even less demagogy. Institutional, public, and private decision-makers, as well as numerous companies, are investing, researching, and developing energy solutions that are in line with the logic of decarbonization. I do not intend to underestimate the efforts that have been made, because they exist. I regularly meet entrepreneurs who are driven by a humanistic spirit characterized by the desire to move our society towards a better world. Do not take them for idealists! These people give themselves the means to realize their projects. In the same way, I salute the efforts of the European institutions and the many associated organizations that support the energy transition and help companies to develop their plans. I remain convinced that the efforts made will pay off and that we will succeed in reducing our dependence on oil and other fossil natural resources... but certainly not in the short term. A transition is not a revolution. It does not imply a brutal wipe-out of something. It is therefore a long-term process. This is precisely what worries me about Antonio Guterres' speech to the United Nations General Assembly. At the rate at which we are consuming and seeing the degradation of our climate, will we have enough time to make an energy transition without first having tipped into a situation of no return? Once again, I deplore the wide gap between common sense and the interests that place oil among the undisputed priorities.

In my analyses, I say it without false modesty, I often hope to be wrong when I am interested in oil. In this case, its era will one day come to an end, but not soon. I dare to make a comparison with one of Tolkien's major masterpieces, *The Lord of the Rings*. Black gold is the "precious" of many people. I know of no equivalent. I postulate that it will remain abundantly used if a new element, not necessarily energy, does not occupy the heart of the political, economic, geopolitical, and strategic concerns of this world. The proof is that its consumption has never ceased to increase except during the Covid-19 health crisis. Yet, for how long has it been claimed that the intensive consumption of oil harms the environment? Several decades. I have already referred to the fact that we are struggling to reduce the share of fossil fuels in the world's energy mix because of the quantitative increase in global needs to be met. In my opinion, this is not a matter of ill will but rather of impotence, because investments in renewable and other programs are growing year after year. [59] They remain insufficient to allow a significant change in the energy model. Unless I am mistaken, it seems to me that global demand for 2023 will be close to one hundred million barrels per day, a statistic that does not suggest a future decline.

I am thinking of all those national economic systems that depend on the hydrocarbon trade. Often, this sector accounts for the bulk of exports and revenues generated. How will these countries manage to deal with the energy transition without unduly penalizing their national economies? Not all of them have the considerable resources of Saudi Arabia or the United Arab Emirates, which aim to diversify their economic model, which they already finance through an extraordinary investment policy. They are turning to tourism, innovation and other promising sectors that require considerable budgets that not all oil producers have. What will happen to them? Some of them are already experiencing great difficulties, such as Venezuela, for various reasons. The possession of abundant reserves of black gold does not guarantee its owner permanent wealth,

---

[59] Sarah Dumeau, *"Transition énergétique : forte hausse des investissements mondiaux en 2022,"* www.lesechos.fr, February 1, 2023

considering once again that it is an exhaustible resource. But when the latter is unable to guarantee its prosperity while the end of what was supposed to ensure it is announced, it will necessarily have to rely on other means of generating income. Not easy... As for the most influential public and private players in the most precious oil, I doubt that they will agree to revenue cuts in the sole name of the fight against climate change or any form of solidarity. Considering their influence on the financial markets and the economic weight they represent for many jurisdictions; they will defend their best interests which converge on high production to maximize profits. This seems logical to me. Similarly, they have first-rate means of pressure at their disposal whenever they feel threatened: relocations, job cuts, and so on. As a rule, one listens to private companies that threaten to leave!

As already discussed in this book, Barack Obama promoted renewable energies at the expense of hydrocarbons... only in appearance. No American statesman would risk compromising himself by attacking the interests of the powerful local oil lobby. Renewable energies yes, but not without a quid pro quo. This shows the considerable importance of this sector of activity, even in the world's leading economic power, which nevertheless has a diversified economic model. Oil brings a lot of satisfaction to Washington, both for its foreign trade and for the deployment and defense of its strategic interests in the world. I refer to economic pragmatism. Will the fight against climate change overcome this economic reality?

The global energy model will evolve. Gradually, other energy sources will gain increasing weight in the global energy mix. In Europe, I have already emphasized the EU's commitment to planning the decarbonization of its economy in the medium term. The *fit for 55* plan calls for a

55% reduction in greenhouse gas emissions by 2030 compared to 1990 levels. The European Council and the European Parliament, co-legislators of this energy law, aim to achieve climate neutrality by 2050, a high but not unattainable goal. Brussels is making the most of this issue, which it sees as a pioneering one. In this way, it hopes to maintain a leading diplomatic influence on the international scene. However, if the Old Continent has every interest in reducing its dependence on oil, since it imports most of its needs, it intends to deploy normative mechanisms to promote the transition to a new energy model as quickly as possible through the transformation of national economies.

For the EU, the stakes are high. The United States-China rivalry sometimes gives the impression that these two giants are battling it out in a global environment devoid of other powers of equivalent stature. To remain in the fold of the major global spheres of influence, the EU has no choice but to act on behalf of the EU-27 and to position itself on issues where it hopes to establish itself as a leader. Climate change seems to be the ideal challenge for the EU to maintain its voice on major international issues, hence its effective commitment to the energy transition. This choice is the result of the consideration of several interests and ideas. I have no doubt that concern for climate change and its consequences dwells the main source of motivation. On the other hand, in addition to seeking to reduce oil imports for economic purposes, the EU expects to produce its own energy to lower its dependence on energy imports. Dependence on something betrays a form of weakness. On the other hand, in an uncertain geopolitical climate, the EU-27 must stand together more than ever. It is said that there is strength in numbers. This is true, but it is not the image that the EU systematically sends out on the international scene. The Brexit has undoubtedly contributed to this internal turmoil. Certain thorny issues are disturbing the peace of the European institutions. Migration policies and the Ukrainian conflict have brought to light disagreements that betray a lack of unwavering unity. In a world where several emerging powers are increasingly asserting themselves, India and Brazil for example, the EU is seeing diplomatic competition intensify. This increased competition risks altering its influence in international relations.

The fight against climate change coincides with one of the main concerns of the United Nations and its Secretary General. On the other hand, recent political news has shown that the positioning on this subject has its share of frustrations in the eyes of its most fervent defenders. The COP 27 organized by Egypt [60] was generally disappointing, except for a last-minute agreement on loss and damage that was supposed to bring more justice for the countries most severely affected by climate disasters. At the end of the event, the United Nations, Germany, and France were bitter. Since the 2015 Paris Agreement, climate COPs have generally not left a lasting impression. Worse, there is a consensus that the goals set in France remain far from the observed reality. Climate diplomacy exists. The UN COPs are like platforms for dialogue that reveal numerous divergences. The law of numbers does not help negotiations. However, when tackling a problem that threatens humanity, one would be tempted to believe that it facilitates discussion. It is necessary to consider the substance and the form. On the substance, all recognize the seriousness of the identified phenomenon. All agree on the principle of determining the means to fight against climate change. On the form, the collegial discussion comes up against another reality. All states want to develop their economies and boost growth. One never deviates from this truth, which demands performance. It inevitably intrudes

---

[60] Author's note: The event was held from November 6 to 18, 2022, in Sharm El Sheikh.

into the discussions because the same results cannot be demanded of everyone. Indeed, not everyone has the same natural resources. Some export, others import. Demographics come into play as well as the level of economic development. If Iceland easily limits its oil needs thanks to the exploitation of geothermal energy, other countries are developing energy models that are in line with sustainable development. On the other hand, it obviously makes no sense to make any comparison with India or China, two demographic behemoths requiring large imports of black gold. Yet the Asian giants are investing massively in independent energy programs others than natural carbon resources. But this does not solve their current dependence on oil and other fossil fuels. They point this out bluntly.

In 2021, at the end of the COP 26 in Glasgow, this reality caught up with the discussions of the moment and conditioned the harshness of the dialogue. However, a global agreement punctuated the conference, well below the initial expectations of its ambitious President Alok Sharma. Images went viral of him looking misty-eyed and desolate. India managed to win a last-minute case on coal and on loss and damage. In sum, the major issue was the exit from coal, which ultimately led to a reduction target. Is India to blame? The country is defending its economic and strategic interests. Its energy needs and consumption are not in line with the targets set to fight climate change. What source of energy can quantitatively replace India's coal-fired needs without penalizing the national economy? When this question is raised, there is a better understanding of the priorities set by the states. Does India hope to make an energy transition and reduce its greenhouse gas emissions? Certainly. The same answer applies to any country. Many spend more than 10% of their GDP on public health because of the ills caused by pollution. This is considerable. Thus, who would refuse to engage in a process aimed at fighting a phenomenon identified as a threat to humanity? I have no doubt about that. However, other influential factors weigh in the balance of decisions. Sometimes, by trying too hard to tackle polluting resources, one induces undesirable effects.

Fossil fuels and their intensive consumption irritate the defenders of environmental causes. I would like to add nuclear power to the list of undesirables. This sector of activity is divisive. I understand the arguments of its detractors and respect them. The atom challenges. It is feared. Three Mile Island, Chernobyl and more recently Fukushima have left their mark as much as their time. Fortunately, nuclear incidents occur exceptionally. The treatment of nuclear waste and its burial are also criticized. In short, many people believe that this activity should be stopped. Germany made this choice a few years ago. Since then, it has reopened coal-fired power plants. The war in Ukraine has not helped. Berlin has temporarily relied on this fossil resource to reduce its dependence on Russian gas. In other words, decarbonization in Germany will wait. I am not criticizing German policymakers. In France, nuclear power is the subject of many political debates, but the global context calls for caution. One knows how to produce electricity thanks to the atom. Despite aging infrastructures, it is possible to extend the life of a nuclear power plant, although such a plan is expensive. This electricity production makes it possible to limit oil imports at a time when the price of oil has an economic impact on its buyers. The national executive makes choices and assumes them.

For my part, I believe that if one cannot make the best decisions, one should look to the least bad ones. In this case, Paris and Berlin share a common desire to decarbonize their national economies. Circumstances and disruptive elements sometimes thwart good will, including that of the actors most determined to turn the page on fossil fuels and oil. The communication from the UN Secretary General does not exaggerate the immensity of the challenge to be met when it refers to climate change. This speech denounces a situation that leads us to fear the worst soon if the results do not follow. No one disputes the general awareness of climate issues, but this is not enough. It requires concrete actions that come up against very counteracting realities, sometimes involuntary, sometimes resulting from strategic choices. However, they do not overshadow the efforts made by the many companies that are researching and developing projects focused on sustainable development.

Reasons to hope for a better world

The French Institute of Petroleum and New Energies (French IFPEN) informs us that the weight of oil in world GDP has declined since the 1980s, from 7% to 3.8% by 2022. [61] This trend can be explained by the desire of public decision-makers and industrialists to turn to another economic model related to energy. The era of cheap oil seems to be over, but let's be careful not to trust appearances! This statistic has its share of truths, but let's not hide the growth of this same global GDP over the last four decades and the considerable increase in the volumes of black gold produced and consumed. I insist on this point because the statistical decline mentioned does not necessarily coincide with a loss of influence in the world economy. The major oil companies have since seen their turnover rise to record levels thanks to the increase in the average selling price per barrel combined with the increase in volumes produced.

In 2022, the context of the war in Ukraine favored the majors' good business, whose net profits amounted to tens of billions of dollars. ExxonMobil took the lead with $55.7 billion in profits. [62] It was followed by Shell (40), BP (27.6), Chevron (35.5) and Total Energies (20.5). [63] These large corporations did not shy away from these fantastic results after several lean years linked to the decline in trading prices that began in 2014. Such results augured good prospects for investments, job creations, dividends that delighted shareholders, and so on. Such economic performances remain rare, all sectors of activity taken

---

[61] *"Réduire l'empreinte carbone de l'industrie : captage, stockage et valorisation du CO2,"* www.ifpenergiesnouvelles.fr, July 15, 2022
[62] Estelle Imbert, *"Qui sont les 5 super majors pétrolières aux bénéfices exceptionnels ?,"* www.forbes.fr, February 10, 2023
[63] *Ibid.*

together. One can imagine that they whet the appetite of many. These exceptional results are not limited to the oil sector alone. It radiates to others who benefit from this success because the money circulates. As for the nationalized companies, the profits generated feed the local economies. The oil giant is becoming an essential sponsor of the system, at the risk of exposing a country to a less bright future when exchange prices fluctuate downwards.

As one reads these lines, many would have no interest in making an energy transition. I do not underestimate the truth of this statement. On the other hand, these actors do not control the world. They can circumvent legislation committed to changing the energy model, the standards of responsible finance (the famous ESG criteria [64]) and other mechanisms intended to contribute to the decarbonization of the world economy. I am banking on the determination of bold entrepreneurs to work on solutions, perhaps transitional ones, that will enable us to reduce our consumption of fossil fuels. I believe this even more because I frequently attend energy conferences where companies present great projects. I would point out that large companies are also looking at innovative solutions that address greenhouse gas emissions. I do not enter the scientific field of engineering, for which I do not have the technical arguments to debate. I confine myself to a more systemic analysis of a global energy market in full evolution. The latter is considering many opportunities for renewable solutions. Companies are vying with each other to present their innovations and their benefits for the environment. I also mention the numerous *smart city* projects, which obviously include an energy dimension. They are defined as *"urban policies using information and communication technologies (ICT) to accelerate the*

---

[64] Author's note: ESG stands for environmental, social and governance criteria.

ecological transition of a city while displaying its international competitiveness." [65] They seek to consume energy differently by optimizing its use and reducing its impact on the environment. Research and development are working to promote future solutions, those that will begin to reduce the world's needs for oil.

I am putting on my party-pooper's light suit, for a few moments only. These good initiatives have their limits. However, they are not prohibitive. Many ambitious companies, especially start-ups, face the problem of project financing. Innovative projects often struggle to raise funds, even when they benefit from the financial support of public banks, European funds and other institutional partners who inject considerable sums that unfortunately prove insufficient for many entrepreneurs who must supplement their economic needs through private investment. I have discovered some great projects on hydrogen, a very fashionable energy that is the focus of many hopes in Europe. Money will continue to be the lifeblood of the industry. Without it, progress is slow, or one resigns oneself to throwing in the towel. In the world of start-ups, all sectors combined, the life expectancy of these young companies does not exceed three years in most cases. The concept and the management of the company are not enough. Projects fail for many reasons, often due to poor management, communication, positioning, or market understanding. The business model does not convince. The business plan is not attractive. Other entities disappear while there are no complaints about their functioning other than not raising the necessary funds. The power of

---

[65] *"Smart city,"* geoconfluences.ens-lyon.fr, September 2017 Original version : *« des politiques urbaines utilisant les technologies de l'information et de communication (TIC) pour accélérer la transition écologique d'une ville tout en affichant sa compétitivité internationale. »*

seduction and conviction with investors has taken on an extraordinary dimension in an ultra-competitive and ever more specialized world of expertise. I also target the gloom or uncertainty that reigns around the circles of investors. Several financial scandals have recently shaken the world. The bankruptcy of FTX and the fall of its founder have dented the reputation of the speculative cryptocurrency world. The collapse of Silicon Valley Bank (SVB) also caused a major earthquake in the world of start-ups and innovation. These two cases have generated a considerable shock wave because they are added to many factors that support the thesis of uncertainty: inflation, war in Ukraine, and so on. However, in such circumstances, the most discerning investors remain on the lookout for good investment opportunities, but they are extremely demanding as to the quality of the dossiers submitted. Finally, there is a lesser-known factor: the administrative authorizations that must be obtained to have the honor of marketing an innovation. These authorizations are usually obtained after many months of waiting. The time factor is generally one of the haunts of the entrepreneur. It proves to be merciless and stressful for anyone who starts the countdown to fundraising.

The search for new energy solutions concerns both large companies and young start-ups. Not all have the same resources to advance their projects. In the energy sector, research and development require substantial budgets, of the order of several million US dollars at least. In this sense, money is the nerve center of any present and future ambition. It is the fuel for companies. Without it, they cease to function.

This economic reality does not hinder the enthusiasm of entrepreneurs who are thinking about the world of tomorrow. Like any builder or founder, these people take risks, but when it comes to the energy transition, I am talking to people who are committed and not just invested in generating economic success. These people genuinely care about the future of the planet. I have already spoken with entrepreneurs who have been offered great deals to buy out their companies but have turned them down because they were suspicious of the true intentions of the alleged buyers. In other words, money is not the only purpose for them. They prefer to earn less but to make sure that the buyer continues the work with the same determination and motivation that characterized their designer. The durability of the project takes precedence over any other interest. These people invest their money, time, and energy to contribute to the fight against climate change. They care about the planet and hope to make a difference. I often find this state of mind when I talk to these entrepreneurs. Aware of the many difficulties that may not allow them to achieve the desired success, they take risks and tackle, on their own scale, the major environmental problems that threaten our societies.

I could cite many examples of companies that are developing fascinating projects to reduce, optimize and even change our energy consumption habits while ensuring that they do not impact the environment. One company caught my attention: Graphenaton Technologies. The website of the French Association of Printed Electronics (AFELIM) presents it as *"the first manufacturer of graphene radiating films dedicated to main heating. It is a Swiss company whose innovation is based on two areas of expertise: mastering graphene applications and mastering printed electronics and power."* [66] I sometimes exchange

---

[66] *Graphenaton*, www.afelim.fr, accessed April 10, 2023 Original version: « *le premier fabricant de films rayonnants au graphène dédiés au chauffage principal. C'est une entreprise suisse dont l'innovation s'appuie sur deux expertises : la maîtrise des applications du graphène*

with its President. I have also met several of its employees, especially the experts working in research and development. I witnessed a demonstration of a patented technology that left the audience speechless, including the energy experts at the event. These radiant films produce energy. They have amazing properties. I see a great future for them in large-scale production because, in addition to the patents filed, Graphenaton is developing technologies that could revolutionize the production and consumption of energy in many areas. These films can be used in the construction industry, in the automotive industry and in the food industry. I am only giving a few examples, but if I refer to the heating problems in France that have arisen due to the war in Ukraine, Graphenaton's radiant films would be an energy solution for households as well as for the French authorities. In the automotive sector, they would replace conventional fuels. As for the agri-food industry, in view of climate change, the company is developing a small technology that would allow crops to be protected from the destructive vagaries of the weather as harvest time approaches. Pierre-Antoine Racine and his teams devote their efforts to the unwavering quest to improve the performance of the technologies they have developed. These technologies are already delivering amazing results.

My Mediterranean origins keep reminding me of the summer heat, the influx of vacationers and the consequences in terms of pollution. A haze reigns during the daytime on the most critical days. Regulars know that it comes from a combination of ambient heat and air pollution. I am equally concerned about the sea. I have not bathed there for many years. Its repulsive dirtiness puts me off. I make a distinction between natural waste from the sea and those resulting from human activity. One does not

---

confuse seaweed with cigarette butts or plastic bottles... Too many incivilities harm marine ecosystems and impact the whole food chain. Scientific studies show that one consumes contaminated fish and other seafood because of human behavior. The Economic, Social and Environmental Council (ESEC) deplores the fact that there is no place on Earth that is free of plastic pollution. [67] As you know, this charming material is nothing other than a product derived from oil.

In 2019, the OECD estimated that only 9% of plastic waste completed their life cycle recycled ... while the same year, the global production reached four hundred and sixty million tons of plastic. [68] Finally, these elements would account for 85% of marine waste. [69] These statistics do not encourage optimism but motivate entrepreneurs who are working hard to raise awareness of marine pollution and seek to develop technologies to reduce its negative effects on the environment.

I had the pleasure of meeting a man involved in this battle. His name is François-Alexandre Bertrand. A sympathetic, passionate, and committed character, he is above all a determined man. He is not content to denounce, he acts. An excellent communicator, he unites people around him and leaves no one unmoved, so much so that his power of persuasion makes an impression. I invite you to learn more about his activities and his current events. This entrepreneur is full of energy. He has been thinking for many years about an innovative technology allowing the collection of plastic waste in the seas. This man has a head

---

[67] *"« Aucun endroit de la planète » épargné : un rapport s'inquiète de l'omniprésence de la pollution plastique,"* www.bfmtv.com, April 11, 2023
[68] *Ibid.*
[69] *Ibid.*

for ideas, and nothing will stop him. He is the President of the Blue Odyssey Initiative, which works to *"protect the seas and oceans by combining technology and people."* [70] He has designed a semi-submersible, the Platyplus Craft, a technological marvel designed to observe pollution in the shallow waters, up to fifteen meters, and to map plastic waste which constitutes the main maritime pollution in the world. He hopes to determine the life cycle of plastic in the sea and to establish an inventory of the seabed. François-Alexandre Bertrand has appeared in various media to present his projects, which may help to clean up the sea. I salute the initiatives of this man sincerely concerned about the degradation of the environment and the future of life on Earth. He deserves to be better known. In addition to his cheerful character, he is full of ideas and defends his convictions like no other. As for the technologies he is developing, they augur a happier future for our seas and oceans. They may allow us to clean up these immense aquatic spaces and preserve the life of the fauna and flora. By exchanging with him, I want to believe that a better world remains possible and that it is not a fantasy or a utopia.

All these examples have a common denominator: an unfailing determination to work for the future of humanity. It goes without saying that one does not develop such a project without expecting economic benefits, but these people have a discourse that moves away from considerations of profitability or the race for profits. There is a fundamentally humanistic and therefore progressive motivation. These people may hold the keys to the future of the Earth. I am not exaggerating in any way. When I see the speed at which technological progress is driving our lives, I would not understand if an innovation did not become the

---

[70] blue-odyssey.org

new standard for sustainable consumption. I refuse to imagine that Man continues to dig his own grave as if it were an inevitability, without trying to equip himself with the means to reverse a trend with prospects that suggest the worst. Not all entrepreneurial projects will lead to the success expected by their founders, but some will certainly experience extraordinary development. I have no doubt that they will contribute to the famous energy transition so desired by the United Nations and its Secretary General Antonio Guterres.

Men and women have marked their time. Inventions have changed our lives. Everything evolves at a very high speed. I was about ten years old when I first heard about the Internet. Three decades later, not only is this technology part of our daily lives, but it has changed many behaviors. My parents' generation probably did not imagine that a technological innovation could have such an impact on our lives. What about the cell phone? I belong to an age group that knew life before the Internet and these small phones that fit in a trouser pocket. I knew the time of the handset, the thick paper directories, or the famous phone booths. All that is now a thing of the past. My children do not know what a VCR is. But they have quickly learned what a Wi-Fi connection can allow to do with. I do not feel like we are just one generation apart. In other publications, I sometimes refer to inventions that were still science fiction not long ago. About ten years ago, in a book on energy, I devoted a chapter to the theme of the conquest of extra-terrestrial resources, starting with those on the Moon. I remember the amused reactions of readers who did not understand the inclusion of such a reflection in a serious study. Nowadays, who would dare to say that it is a fantasy? The conquest of space has seen entrepreneurs invest considerable sums of money in the development of projects that strive to push the limits of what is possible. Robert Bigelow, Jeff Bezos, Elon

Musk, Richard Branson, and others embody this entrepreneurial spirit that nobody dares to discriminate. We do not associate these names with crazy projects; on the contrary, when they speak on the subject, they embody innovation and progress. They are called pioneers or visionaries. Why should not other entrepreneurs succeed in designing the clean energy that will lead to the end of oil use?

Conclusion

As I come to the end of my reflection, the first thought that comes to my mind is about the legacy we will leave to our children. What will we leave them? Everyone is free to believe or not in the climate change thesis. For my part, I rely on the studies produced by climate experts and their reports worry me. The studies carried out by the IPCC highlight a trend that seems to become more pronounced every year. They denounce a situation for which they recommend urgent action. Oil consumption is one of the factors contributing to this climatic phenomenon with alarming consequences on the environment.

Critics argue that there is insufficient evidence to support a correlation between the global rise in temperature and oil consumption. I, for one, see an analogy between the two. As already evoked, since the international community has been seriously concerned about the future of the climate, it has seen a steady increase in its consumption of oil. It would be a misjudgment to attribute the entire responsibility for climate change to this precious oil, and more generally to fossil fuels, but I am firmly convinced that human action plays a major role in global warming.

A big gap remains between *want* and *can*. When we talk about the imperative need to reduce oil consumption in the world, two major questions must be raised: do we want to and can we? To the first question, I oppose a Norman answer. Yes and no. To the second, I will stick to a nuanced statement.

When we discuss oil and the desire to reduce our dependence on this natural resource, it goes without saying that there is a sincere desire to move in this direction, including among public decision-makers. There is a real willingness in some institutional spheres to engage in the path of the post-oil era. The planet is suffering. We consume its natural resources to excess. Not only are we plundering it, but as soon as we are dealing with exhaustible resources, what will happen the day they have been fully exploited? Black gold is obviously one of the exhaustible resources. I note above all that we have exploited and consumed incredibly high volumes of natural resources in a century compared to the last centuries or even millennia. This statement does not only apply to oil. Of course, demographics, industrialization, economic performance, and other factors explain this growing need for raw materials. Mother Nature has a tolerance threshold and reminds us of it when we abuse her kindness. The consequences of climate change are of great concern. The United Nations regularly draws everyone's attention to a reality in the making, that of climate refugees who will number in the hundreds of millions in the coming decades. The habitable surface on Earth will tend to shrink. This seems unavoidable. Similarly, climate change has its share of nuisances causing large-scale economic damage. I could give other reasons why policymakers are moving towards decarbonizing the global economy. There is talk of the ultimate threat to life on our planet. We are already seeing disturbing impacts on many ecosystems. We should therefore be encouraged to act as quickly as possible and to put in motion all possible and imaginable means to try to counter this fatal trend as predicted by the scientific world and so often taken up by the United Nations.

The threats to life on Earth do not carry as much weight as other issues that continue to drive the political and economic agenda of the world. Oil embodies wealth, power, and the ultimate leverage for those who can threaten anyone with cutting off their supplies and making them vulnerable. Without oil, a country is powerless. Armies and the entire societal system are paralyzed. As soon as a disturbing rumor about black gold arises, the world holds its breath, and the financial markets go wild. I am hardly exaggerating, but this natural resource remains at the heart of the concerns of the world's major public and private decision-makers. It remains a key element of the global economy. How many goods and services require its use to produce and satisfy them?

On the other hand, it is never far from the great power games. Even nuclear power does not inspire such cold sweats. The world fears the use of the atom, especially for military purposes, but it is mostly described as a means of deterrence and neutralization. Once the major powers have it, everyone knows where they stand. This does not apply to oil, because the big powers do not fight in the same weight category. I make the following dichotomy: those who possess opulent reserves and those who seek to secure their supplies. Thus, if nuclear force has a much greater destructive power, oil is the weapon with which one impacts the adversary to suffocate him internally by attacking his economic model.

As for the power to make a difference, again, I cannot give a definitive answer. In a world where technological and scientific advances are moving at great speed, I remain optimistic that we will be able to make a successful energy transition. I believe in it. There is no shortage of projects with great prospects. Entrepreneurs are working to find and develop the solutions of tomorrow. The initiatives are there. However, I hope that they will not come up against conflicting interests that will act as obstacles to their promotion. On the other hand, when I look at the world oil consumption, I find it difficult to imagine an energy transition towards cleaner energies in the short term. My concern is mainly with the scientific opinions that urge the international community to reduce its dependence on fossil fuels as soon as possible. Between the urgency of action and what we can offer in the way of immediate sustainable solutions, I perceive a gap, something akin to an incompatibility of the moment. Do not see any provocation on my part, but it will probably take many years for sustainable and clean energies to take the ascendancy over traditional energy resources that have an impact on the environment. I only ask to be wrong and that someone brings me the proof that a successful energy transition is possible in the medium term, that the world manages in fine to consume more cleanly. I dream of the day when the message will circulate that we are on the right track.

As I finish this book, I cannot help but return to a significant event of the beginning of 2023 that was briefly discussed in this book. China has just pulled off a resounding diplomatic tour de force by bringing Iran and Saudi Arabia together around a discussion table. The meeting naturally took place in Beijing. This normalization of relations between these two rival oil producers has generated the effect of a thunderclap in the Western world. The Wahhabi kingdom preferred to negotiate with China and not with its traditional Western allies. Washington got the message. This is a real diplomatic slap in the face for the White House and the State Department. It also shows once again that China expects to increase its political influence in the world, much to the chagrin of the United States, although there is no guarantee that the agreement will be sustainable. On the other hand, while oil alone does not explain Beijing's motives for reconciling the Iranians and Saudis, its name was likely mentioned repeatedly in the preparatory meetings for this diplomatic meeting. Anxious to secure his country's supplies of black gold, Xi Jinping has just pulled off a master stroke by easing the atmosphere between two of its main suppliers. Not only has he managed to re-establish a dialogue between two rival states, but he has also ensured a certain tranquility regarding the strategic passage of the Strait of Hormuz and oil freight to China. By inviting Tehran and Riyadh to renew contact, Beijing may have initiated a new diplomatic era in the Middle East, especially in the areas of crisis where the two former enemies have long been at odds. How can we not cite the case of the war in Yemen? The Wahhabi kingdom supports the government in Sana'a while Iran defends the Houthi rebels who regularly carry out attacks against the Saudi neighbor. Oil infrastructures are among the preferred targets of Houthi attacks. Any incident affecting this type of installation would immediately provoke a cascade of reactions around the world, starting with the financial markets, which would be set ablaze by the potential consequences. As for China, it is especially important that nothing disrupts its supply networks from the Persian Gulf.

The most recent news shows once again that oil is never far from the concerns at the heart of major diplomatic and strategic maneuvers. It always occupies a place of the first order in the great world game. In a state of competition, be it political, economic or of any other nature, one systematically seeks to weaken the competitor. Black gold still holds the prize for being the most effective pressure tactic when there is a threat of supply disruptions. For the time being, I cannot imagine it disappearing from the great international intrigues any time soon. For this reason, its world consumption will remain high, because a significant drop in its demand would immediately lead to a loss of its influence as a means of pressure. I therefore postulate that this is not the desired effect of those who hold this asset that can thwart the interests of their rivals. I am referring to the great political and economic opposition between the United States and China.

In another book, I wrote at length about ESG criteria [71] which have become central to responsible investment and sustainable development in recent years. I defended the thesis that beyond the responsible consideration acting as a driving force justifying or not investments, it seemed to me that these criteria constitute a subtle political weapon against competing states or foreign companies. A news item made public in October 2020 had particularly caught my attention. A large American investment fund had declared that it would not invest in Russia, China, and Saudi Arabia. [72] By naming these three countries, I understood that ESG criteria were being used beyond the only responsible dimension.

Through standards that are in fact nebulous, it is easy to penalize a competitor by saying that it does not respect human rights sufficiently, that its governance is too opaque or that it pollutes too much. I can multiply the examples: when one wants to prevent a competitor from raising the necessary funds, one will always find a way to expose grievances justifying the refusal of investment. I consulted several documents published by auditing companies concerning studies on companies in the international oil industry and the scores obtained by these companies regarding ESG criteria. Comparing the 2020 [73] ratings of the American, Russian, Chinese, and Saudi companies on the list, it appeared that no country stood out. All were rated as having high or severe "ESG risk,"

---

[71] Thierry Pastor, *The Dark Power: The New Weapons*, May 19, 2022, 235 p.

[72] Natasha Doff, Selcuk Gokoluk, *"Top Fund's Blacklist Shows ESG Coming for Emerging Markets,"* www.bloomberg.com, October 16, 2020

[73] Author's note: www.sustainalytics.com was accessed when the October 16, 2020, news story was published about this investment fund saying it was placing Russia, China, and Saudi Arabia on an investment blacklist.

regardless of the country or origin of the company. At the time, one question haunted my mind: would U.S. investment funds refuse to invest in U.S. oil and gas companies because of ESG criteria? Three years later, I still wonder.

In 2021, the oil industry suffered a major crisis that precipitated the closure of many American companies. Many of them faced major economic difficulties. I do not know if some of them turned to investment funds for project financing... but since the arrival of shale oil on the international markets and the turmoil caused to conventional oil producers, the United States has never stopped maintaining a high production policy to push down the exchange prices. The more the prices fell, the more they favored the interests of American companies. I would like to remind you once again that this policy on shale oil was promoted by Barack Obama, who was an ardent defender of the fight against climate change and of the 2015 Paris Climate Agreement. Donald Trump continued this production policy by betting on accessible oil at low prices for the end consumer. Such a configuration would also impact the domestic economies of other major competing producers. As for Joe Biden, he promised to tackle black gold production and reduce it... for a somewhat different reality. In fact, in March 2023, Washington urged OPEC to increase production to bring supply more in line with demand. [74] This demand was justified for economic, geopolitical, and strategic reasons, which once again seem to take precedence over the desire to combat global warming. I have already touched on all of this, but the American choices in terms of oil production illustrate the complexity of this world torn between common sense and reason, which call for an effective decarbonization of the

---

[74] *"Les États-Unis réclament à l'Opep une augmentation de la production de pétrole,"* www.latribune.fr, March 7, 2023

world economy, and political and economic pragmatism, which almost always takes precedence.

I conclude this reflection on oil by keeping a positive note regarding projects developed by entrepreneurs who are looking for tomorrow's energy solutions, those that aim to reduce our dependence on this oil that is so precious for the reasons explained in this book. Moreover, even if I persist in believing that the oil era will not end with the depletion of its reserves, the day when other energy sources will have the wind in their sails will necessarily come. The global energy model will evolve and will tend to reduce our dependence on oil. Hydrogen has the ideal profile to become a dominant energy in the future, but who can be sure of future consumption habits? Similarly, I still wonder if the day oil loses its influence in international relations and its intrigues, something else will have to replace it as a means of pressure par excellence. Will it be a mineral, a technology such as artificial intelligence, the production of a virus from a laboratory or perhaps some other unexpected or unsuspected factor? This fossil material has certainly marked its time. No other natural resource has had such an impact on international relations and the global economy.

It is now time for me to address you, oil. Allow me to be so familiar with you, but since I have been writing about you for so long, I have allowed myself this discretionary coquetry. At the mere mention of your name, men lose their minds. Yet, when I see you in your raw state, I do not detect anything that puts you at an advantage. You are smelly. You do not arouse ecstasy by the color you give off. But some know that you have many qualities. The expression "oil king" does not exist by chance. You have allowed some to build huge fortunes. You have caused the distress of many people. People still fight, betray, and kill for you. How many people have sadly lost their lives because of the human folly generated by the importance you are still given? Nowadays, we denigrate you. Your excessive consumption harms our environment. You are put in the dock, but you cannot defend yourself. Don't be afraid! White knights continue to bet on you. They abound in the official discourse, the agreed one that militates for an energy transition in which you will inevitably lose your status of undisputed star of natural resources. However, I think that your end of reign has not yet sounded. You still have a usefulness and an interest which means that, despite the criticism of you, you will not suddenly disappear from the political and economic radar, from the rivalries between the main dominant state powers of this world or from the interests defended by so many public and private companies for whom you are so important. For my part, I do not blame you. Better, I do not hate you because Man remains the only one responsible for his own ills. I pity him because he is sick. He suffers from an addiction. To cure it, he would have to stop giving priority to "higher" interests over the reason that alerts him to the difficult future that is coming for our planet. As distressing as it may seem, I always come back to this famous Hobbesian vision which postulates that *"man is wolf to man."* The day you lose influence in the great issues of this world, something else will become the new force in international relations and the world economy. One day, you will join the memories of History. Time passes. Each era knows its share of evolutions, but one element will not change: Man.

Glossary of abbreviations

AFELIM : Association française de l'électronique imprimée, French association of printed electronics

AFP : Agence France Presse

AUKUS: Australia, United Kingdom, United States

BP: British Petroleum, a hydrocarbon major formerly known as the Anglo-Persian Oil Company and then the Anglo-Iranian Oil Company. For a while, the famous acronym even stood for "Beyond Petroleum".

CIA: Central Intelligence Agency

CNPC: China National Petroleum Corporation

COP: for *Conventions of Parties*, refers to the conferences of signatory states and the supreme body of certain international conferences, including the UN Framework Convention on Climate Change.

EAEC: European Atomic Energy Community

ECSC: European Coal and Steel Community

EEC: European Economic Community, ancestor of the European Union

EIA: Energy Information Administration

ENI : Ente Nazionale Idrocarburi

ESEC: Economic, Social and Environmental Council

ESG: this acronym stands for environmental, social and governance criteria.

EU: European Union

FBI: Federal Bureau of Investigation

FRG: Federal Republic of Germany

GDP: Gross Domestic Product

GDR: German Democratic Republic

IAEA: International Atomic Energy Agency

ICT: Information and Communication Technologies

IEA: International Energy Agency

IFPEN : Institut Français du Pétrole Énergies Nouvelles, French Institute of Petroleum and New Energies

INSEE: Institut national de la statistique et des études économiques, National Institute of Statistics and Economic Studies

IPCC: Intergovernmental Panel on Climate Change

LNG: liquefied natural gas

MI6: Military Intelligence, section 6. Foreign Intelligence Service also known as the Secret Intelligence Service.

MICA Center: Maritime Information Cooperation and Awareness Center

NASA: National Aeronautics and Space Administration

NATO: North Atlantic Treaty Organization

OECD: Organization for Economic Cooperation and Development

OPEC: Organization of the Petroleum Exporting Countries

SVB: Silicon Valley Bank

UN: United Nations

UNCLOS: United Nations Convention on the Law of the Sea

USSR: Union of Soviet Socialist Republics

VCR: Video Cassette Recording

WTI: West Texas Intermediate is a crude oil produced in the United States. It is used as a standard for crude oil pricing.

WWF: formerly World Wildlife Fund, now World Wild Fund for Nature.